HOW-TO DICTIONARY

Written by Marie Shirer
Illustrated by Marla G. Stefanelli

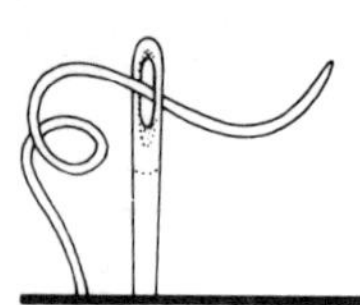

To our mothers, Viola Nelson Shirer and Madelyn Short Gibbs, who taught us to sew with love and patience, gave us the confidence to follow our dreams, and instilled in us the curiosity to "look it up."

This book would not have been possible without the resources offered by the staff and back-issue files of Quilter's Newsletter Magazine. *We would like to thank Bonnie Leman, the magazine's editor-in-chief, and the entire staff of* QNM *for their generous sharing of expertise. . . . Marie Shirer and Marla G. Stefanelli*

The cover was designed and made by Marla G. Stefanelli.

Leman Publications, Inc.
6700 West 44th Avenue
Wheat Ridge, Colorado 80033

Manufactured in the United States of America.
Library of Congress 91-061788
ISBN 0-943721-09-1
First printing 1991
Second printing 1992
Third printing 1992
Fourth printing 1993
Fifth printing 1994

Preface

When preparing to travel to a new and exciting part of the world, people usually take with them a handy, small-size dictionary or phrase book. With such a book tucked conveniently in a purse or pocket, tourists can begin enjoying their adventures immediately upon arrival. When seeing a sign or hearing a word they don't yet know, they can look it up quickly without missing any of the fun. Even experienced travelers, who may have visited a favorite country many times, often want to look up new words and phrases or refresh their memories.

Quiltmakers, whether beginners or seasoned "tourists," set out on a new adventure with each quilting project. This little dictionary is the guidebook for quiltmakers. In it you will find the words that form the language of quilting, those that will be encountered in quilting magazines, patterns, and books. Forming the content of this how-to dictionary are the words that we quiltmakers call our own, terms that are tossed about at guild meetings and workshops to help us communicate about quilts–even though these same words may mean something entirely different to the rest of the world. The entries found here are more than mere definitions–often they clarify a technique or describe a process.

Because this is a book for quilters traveling in a busy world, in it you will read short definitions rather than lengthy explanations. You will discover a lot of good information as you look up words as well as plenty of hidden treasure while leafing through the pages. And, because a picture often is worth a thousand words, we have included a bounty of illustrations to complement the definitions.

So, add this little guidebook to your sewing gear (don't forget your thimble) and have fun on your next quilting adventure, wherever and whatever it may be.

A

Accuracy: the quality of being precise in matching seams and in other quiltmaking techniques. While quilts made for competition may require all the accuracy that is humanly possible to win a top prize, unnecessary worrying about accuracy could spoil the fun of quiltmaking.

Allover Pattern

Acid-Free Tissue Paper: a special paper used for wrapping quilts for storage and (when crumpled) for cushioning folds to prevent creasing.

Album Quilts: friendship or sampler quilts that often are made from one-of-a-kind appliqué blocks. One type of album quilt is the Baltimore Album, an elegant style from the mid-19th century.

Allover Set

All-White Quilts: see White-on-White Quilts.

Allover Pattern: a quilt design that does not use repeated blocks, but rather is made from units or repeated patches.

Allover Set: a quilt design that requires a special arrangement of blocks to make the pattern.

Alternating Blocks

Alternating Blocks: two blocks that vary in some way, whether with different frames, patterns, or fabrics. Such blocks are sewn alternately to make a checkerboard repeat.

Amish Quilts: a term used to describe quilts made by Amish people; also, an identifiable style of quilt made by the Amish up through the early 20th cen-

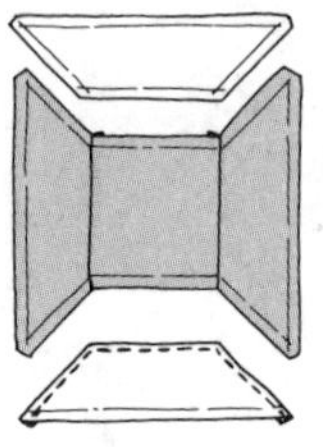

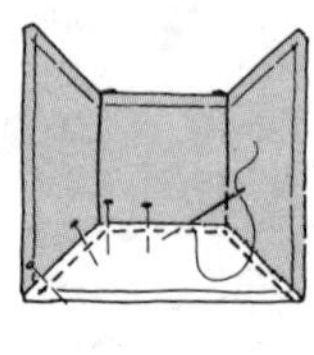

Appli-Piecing

Example of an Appliqué Design

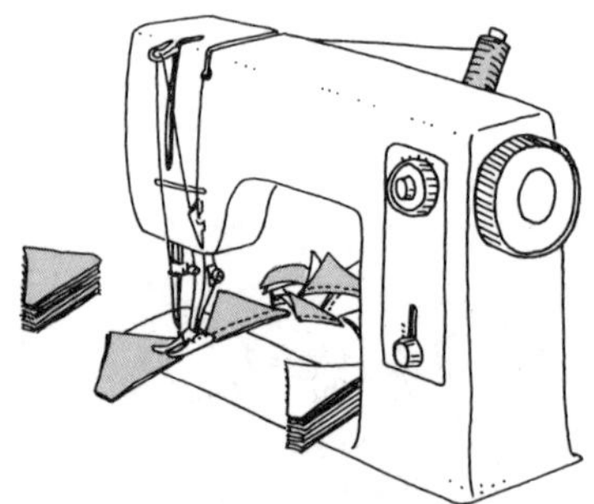

Assembly-Line Piecing

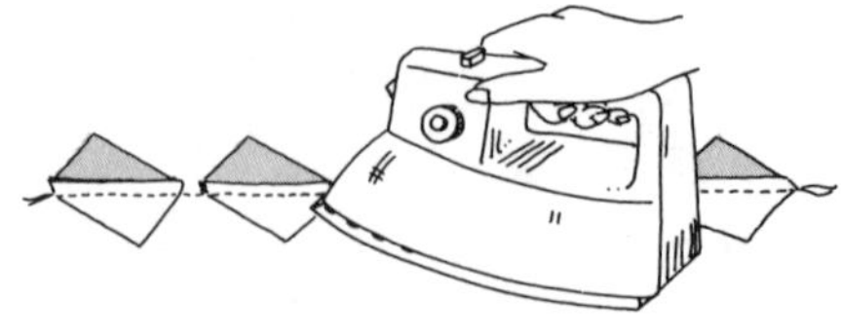

tury. This design style is enjoying popularity among many quiltmakers today. These so-called Amish quilts are typically made in bold geometric patterns with solid-color fabrics in vibrant colors and elaborate quilting.

Angled Seam: see Set-In Seam.

Antiquing Fabric: see Tea Dyeing.

Appli-Piecing: a technique of piecing a block by applying one patch to another in the manner of appliqué and sewing it on the right side with a blind stitch. Appli-piecing is helpful when fabric designs must match precisely.

Appliqué: to sew patches onto a background fabric with hand sewing or machine stitching. Appliquéd patches are often curved; curved patches are usually (but not always) indicative of an appliquéd quilt. Appliqué designs often represent motifs from nature or form a fabric "painting."

Appraisal: a written valuation of a quilt by a certified appraiser that can be used for insurance purposes.

Assembly-Line Piecing: an efficient and fast process for joining patches by machine. Patches are cut and stacked in correct sewing order and all necessary supplies are conveniently placed next to the sewing machine. Patches are joined with chain piecing and are pressed in groups to conserve time and effort.

Autograph Quilts: those that are

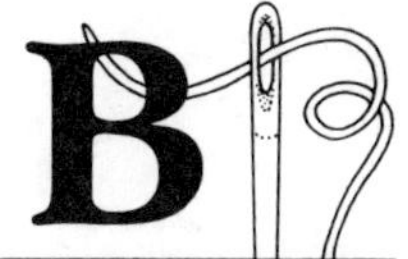

signed (usually by many people) in embroidery or permanent ink. Such quilts can be made to commemorate an event or a friendship, or they might be made as fund raisers by charging a fee for each signature.

Example of an Autograph With Permanent Ink

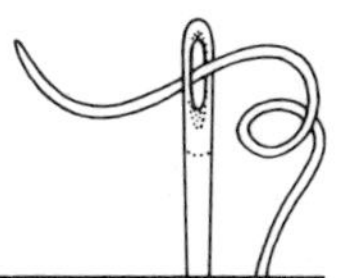

Background Fabric: the material (whether print or solid) on which appliqué patches are sewn; the background fabric of an appliqué block is usually cut the finished block size plus seam allowances. Background fabric also can refer to the fabric chosen for pieced-block patches that appear to recede, thereby allowing other fabrics and patches to form the design.

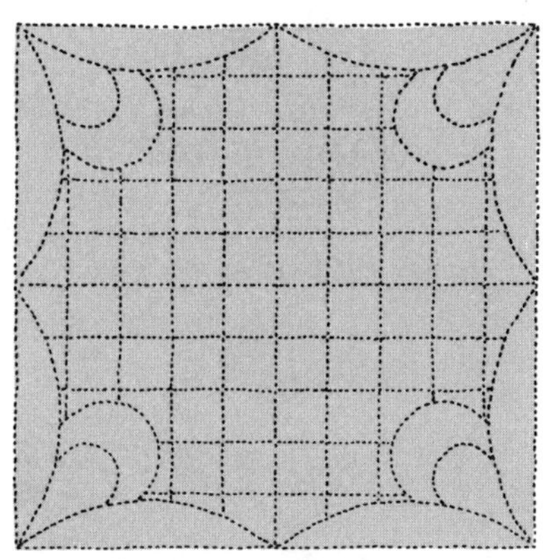

Background (Filler) Quilting

Background (Filler) Quilting: an allover design, often horizontal and vertical or diagonal straight lines, that fills in the background around appliqué or quilting motifs.

Backing: see Lining.

Backstitch: in machine sewing, to sew in reverse over previous stitching to strengthen the beginning or end of a seam. In hand piecing, backstitching refers to two or more stitches on top of each other at the beginning or end of a seam. In hand quilting, to take one or two stitches on top of the last stitch as a method for ending a line of quilting.

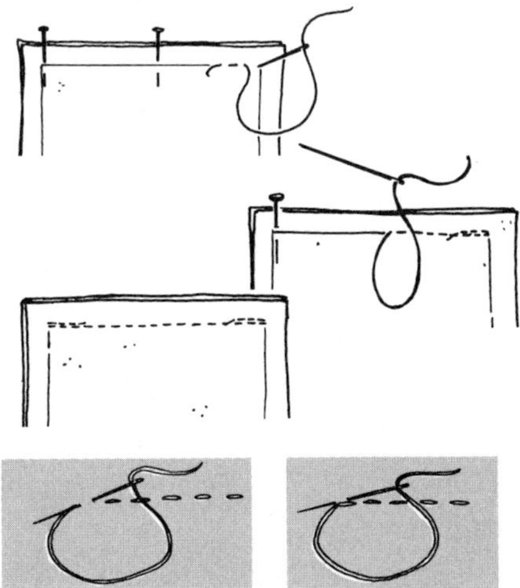

Backstitch

Bag Balm: ointment used to soothe cow udders and sore quilting fingers. It

B

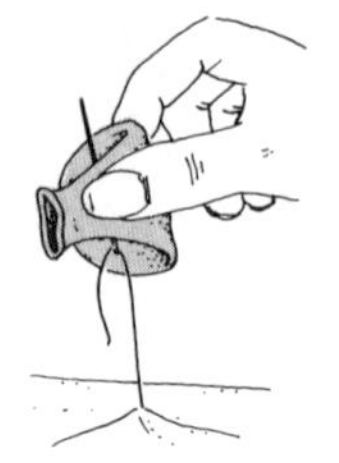
Balloon Used to Pull a Needle

Example of a Baltimore Album Block

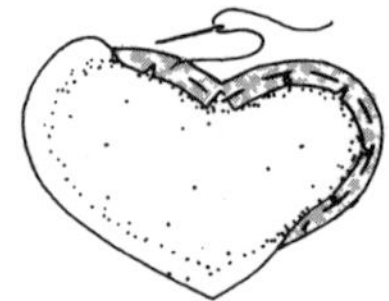
Basting an Appliqué Patch

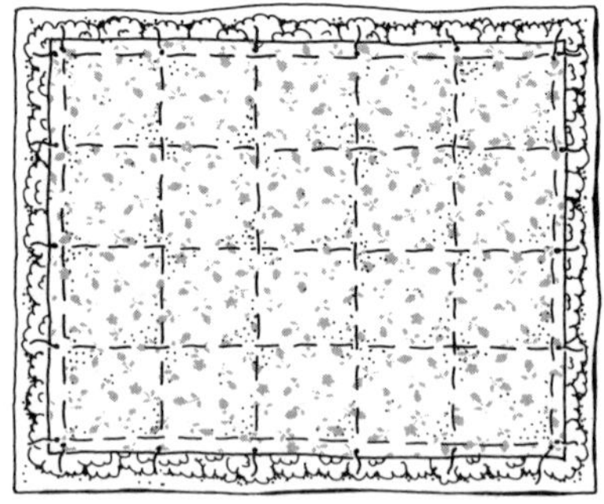
Basting the Layers of a Quilt

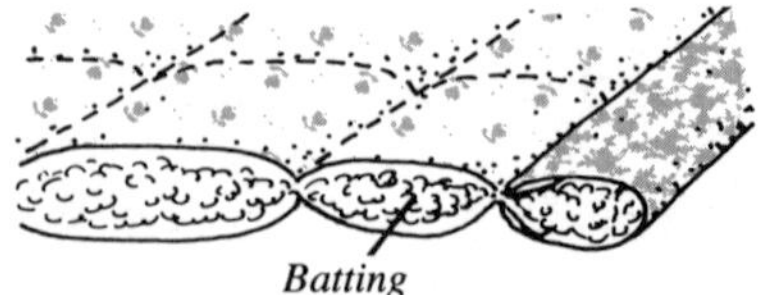

is available at farm-supply stores and quilt shops.

Balloon: when uninflated, a handy thing to use in pulling a needle through a quilt. Tying a quilt through many layers can be a little difficult; using an uninflated balloon to grip the needle will help.

Baltimore Album Quilts: one particular group of album quilts made around Baltimore, Maryland, during the mid-19th century. These quilts typically have elaborate appliqué work with a different design in each block. Fabrics used for the appliqué patches are often bright; the background is usually off-white.

Basting: (1) temporary stitches to hold patches or turn-under allowances in place while the final sewing is done. Basting should be done in thread to match the patch or in light-colored thread so that no marks are left. Basting is removed after the final sewing has been completed.

Basting: (2) the fastening of layers of a quilt (lining, batting, and quilt top) with long running stitches in preparation for tying or quilting. The basting stitches can be about 2″ long in lines that are typically about 6″ apart and run horizontally and vertically across the quilt.

Batting: the filler or middle layer of the quilt. Batting can be made from polyester, cotton, wool, or silk fibers; a majority of quiltmakers today use

batting made of polyester or polyester/cotton blend. Most batting is white although black polyester batting and off-white cotton batting are available. Wool batting is naturally off-white. Choosing the most appropriate batting for a quilt is very important. Thick or "fat" batting is best for tied quilts; most unbonded or cotton batting must be quilted closely (about every one to two inches) to prevent shifting and bunching. New battings continue to appear on the market; quilt-shop personnel can advise about batting selection.

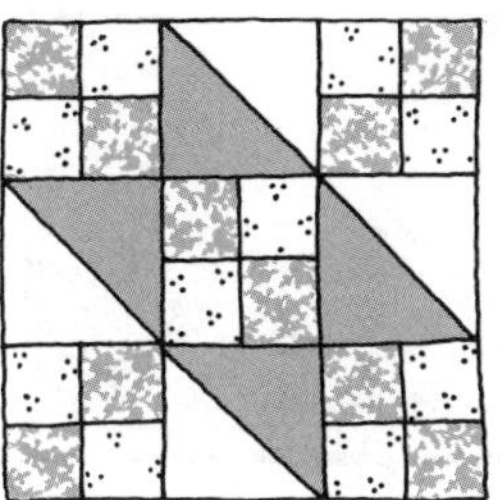

Examples of Good Designs for a Beginner

Bearding: migration of batting fibers through the quilt lining or quilt top. Bearding is particularly noticeable on dark solid fabric, and the problem may be worse when polyester fabrics are used.

Beeswax: a product sold in quilting and fabric shops for coating sewing thread (before quilting) to make it strong and smooth. Quilting thread does not usually require beeswax.

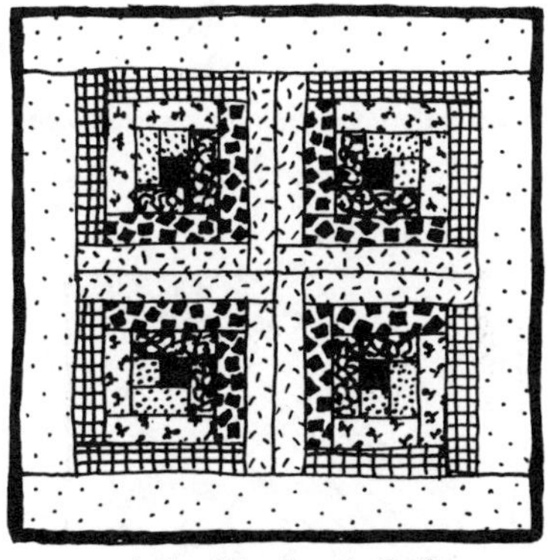

A Good Beginner's Quilt: Log Cabin Blocks With a Simple Border

Beginner's Quilt: a project that will not overtax the skills of a novice quiltmaker and cause discouragement. Good patterns include (but are not limited to) those that have no more than about 30 patches per block and angles of 90° or 45°. The most important consideration, however, is that the quiltmaker love the pattern and fabric.

Between: a short needle with a small eye that is used for hand quilting. Betweens are commonly available in sizes 7-10 and 12; the higher the

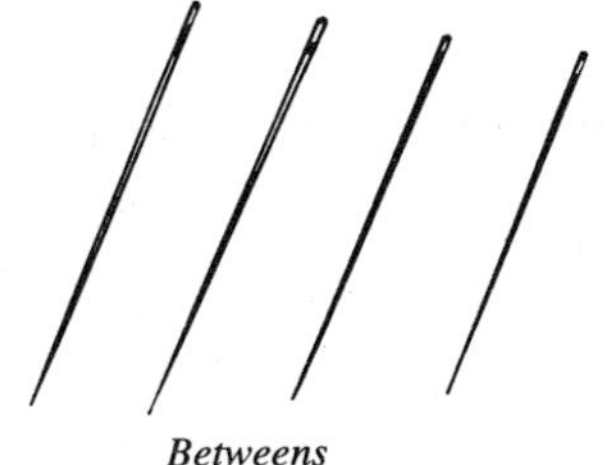

Betweens

B

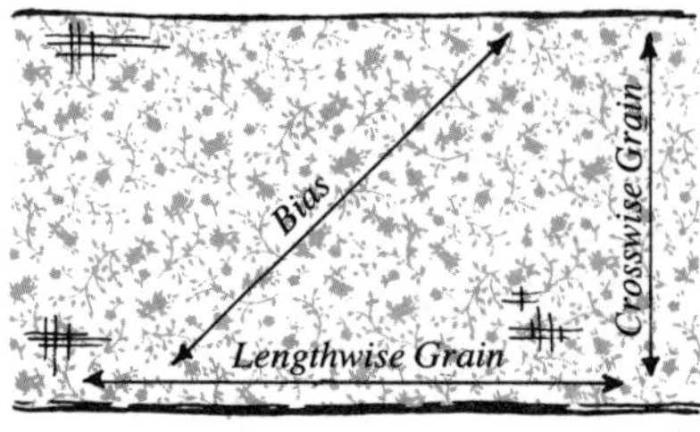

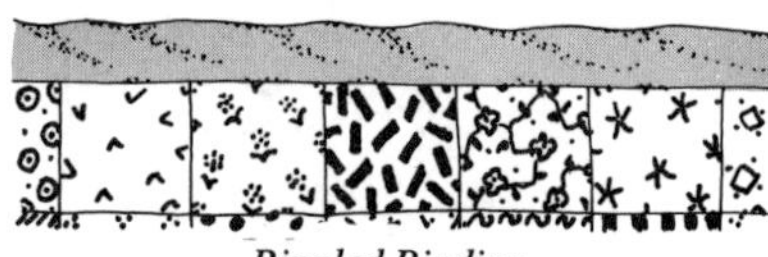
Rippled Binding

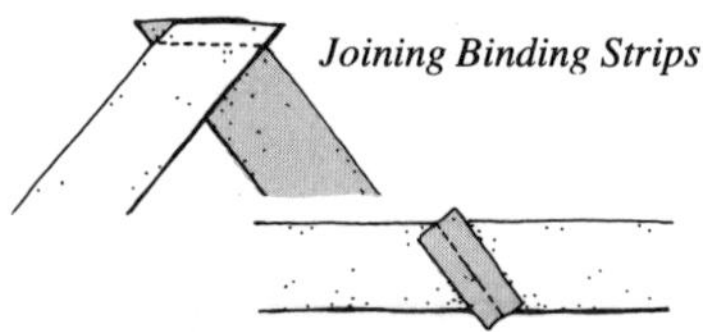
Joining Binding Strips

Seam Allowances Can Be Pressed Open

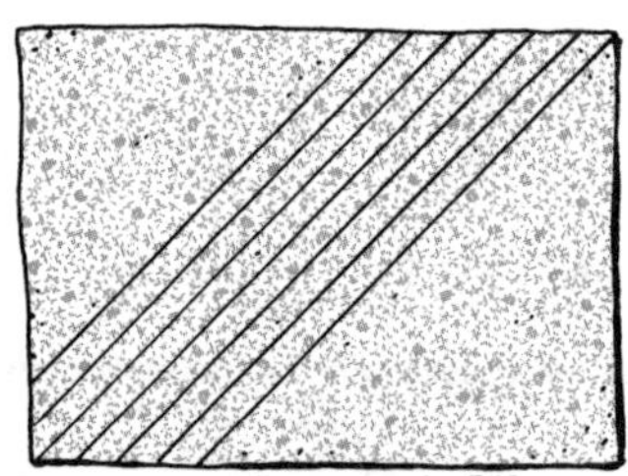
Bias Stripping Marked on Fabric

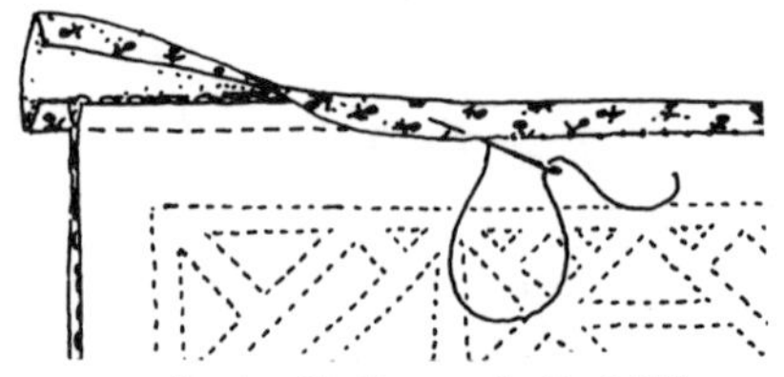
Sewing Binding on the Back Side

number, the smaller the needle.

Bias: the diagonal in relation to the lengthwise and crosswise grain. Bias has considerable stretch. Careful handling in sewing and pressing will prevent problems caused when bias edges stretch out of shape.

Bias Binding: binding cut on the diagonal of the fabric grain. Bias has considerable stretch that is helpful when binding a quilt with rounded corners or curved edges, but that same stretch can ripple and crawl unless care is taken when attaching the binding and sewing it on the back side. The longest piece of bias binding that can be cut from 44″-wide fabric is about 60″, so you will need several seams joining the lengths of binding. Cutting strips from full-width fabric allows a minimal number of seams. Diagonal seams joining the strips allow the binding to be as flat as possible.

Bias Stripping: long, narrow pieces of fabric cut on diagonal grain. Bias stripping is usually cut with a rotary cutter. It frequently is used for appliquéd stems and similar design elements, and many quiltmakers use it for binding.

Binding: a strip of fabric, either bias or straight-grain, used to encase the edges of a quilt. The binding is sewn on after the quilt has been quilted or tied. It can be made from one continuous strip of fabric or each edge of the quilt can be bound with a separate binding strip. Binding can finish any width from narrower than ¼″ to about an inch, but ⅜″ is the most common finished size.

Biscuit (Puff) Quilting: a construction technique of making small stuffed pillows (puffs) and joining them to create a comforter.

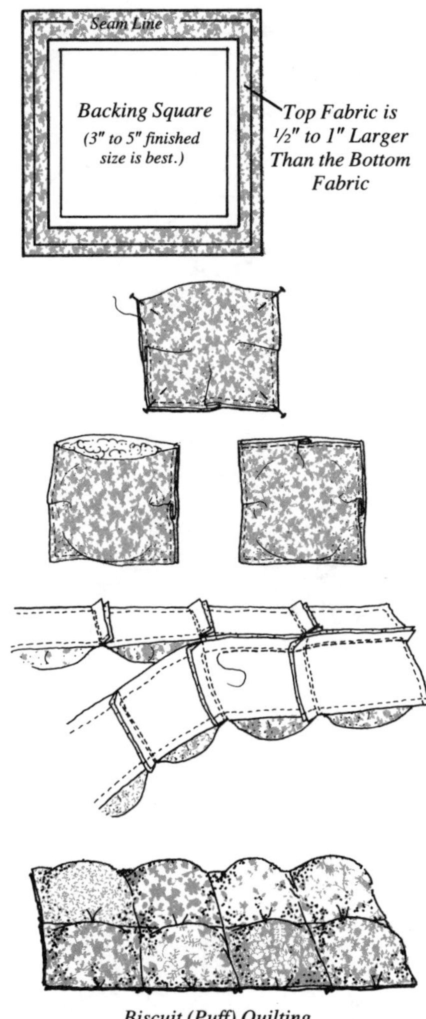

Biscuit (Puff) Quilting

Bleeding: the loss of dye when fabric gets wet. This fugitive dye can stain other fabrics, and fabrics that bleed may be noticeably lighter after several washings. It is generally recommended that quiltmakers test each fabric by soaking it (or a scrap of it) in hot water, perhaps with a little soap. If the dye bleeds, continue rinsing until water remains clear. Occasionally you may find a fabric that will not stop bleeding. It may be best to discard that fabric rather than risk using it in a quilt.

Blends: fabrics made of more than one fiber, such as cotton and polyester. Blends usually do not hold a crease as well as all-cotton fabric; for this reason they often are not the first choice of quiltmakers.

Blind Stitch: the most often used method of sewing appliqués in place by hand. Blind stitch leaves only a tiny spot of thread showing on the front of the quilt. Stitches generally should be no farther apart than ⅛″.

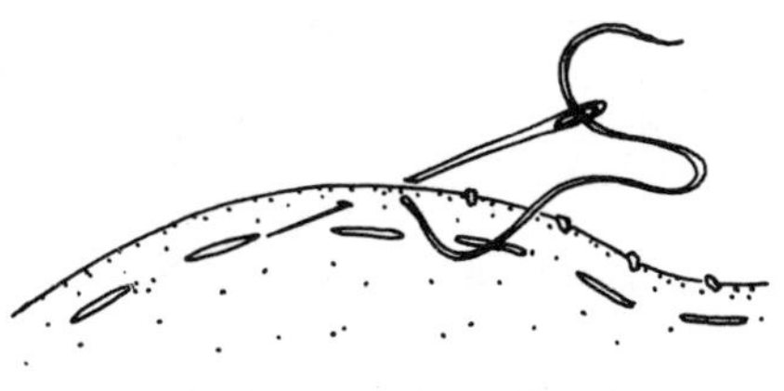
Blind Stitch (Enlarged Detail)
Also Shown: Basting for Turn-Under Allowances

Block: a design unit, usually a square, that is repeated to make the quilt top. Most quilts are made with blocks although there are other methods for constructing quilt tops (see Allover

B

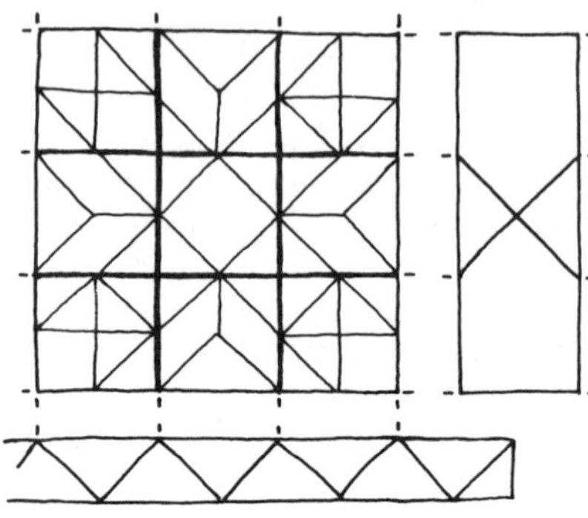

Block Divisions

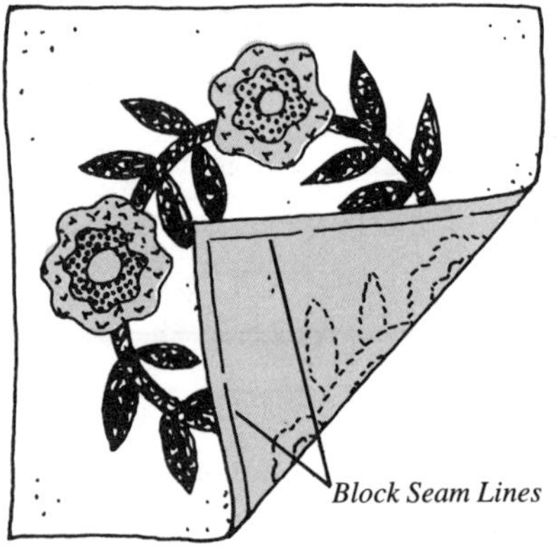

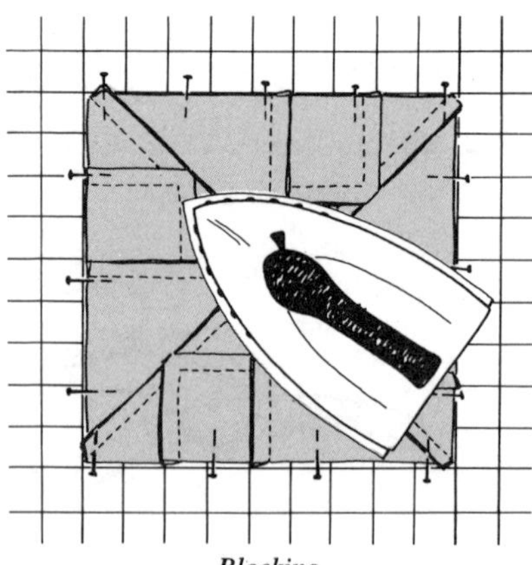

Blocking

Pattern). The blocks usually are made first and then are sewn together with other parts of the quilt top. The block style of quiltmaking became popular in the United States in the early 1800s.

Block Divisions: the major block seam lines. Many pieced blocks are designed to have equal or proportional divisions. Studying a block's divisions is the first step in drafting a pattern. One easy way to plan pieced sashing is to divide the sashing with seams that match some or all of the block divisions. Likewise, pieced borders can be planned with patches that will align with some or all of the block divisions.

Block Seam Lines: markings on the wrong side to indicate the finished edges of the quilt block. If the block seam lines are marked on the front side of the quilt block by mistake (which can happen particularly on appliquéd blocks), very careful sewing will be required to be sure the marked lines do not show after the stitching is completed.

Blocking: gently pulling and pinning a block (or other unit) into its intended shape and steaming it. Seam allowances can be pressed at the same time, especially if the blocking is done wrong side up.

Blood Stains: the occasional result of pricking your finger while quilting. One popular helpful hint quilters enjoy is that you can spit on a blood stain to remove it because saliva will effectively dissolve the blood. Cold water, with or without a little detergent, also will probably work in removing a spot of fresh blood.

Bonded Batting: polyester batting that has a heat-set resin or glaze coating. Bonding (also called glazing) controls bearding and produces batting that need not be quilted as closely (perhaps every 6″) as unbonded-polyester or natural-fiber batting.

Schoolhouse Blocks With Borders

Border: the outer area of the quilt (inside the binding), much like a frame on a picture. Borders can be made from any number of plain strips of fabric, or they can be pieced or appliquéd. Most quilts have borders although some do not. Borders can be very wide, very narrow, or any width in between; a quilt can have more than one border.

Border Print: fabric with patterned design bands printed along the lengthwise grain. Some border prints have one border; others have many repeated borders. Border prints often coordinate with other allover-print fabrics.

Border Print

Bride's Quilt: any quilt made for a bride, but particularly an album or friendship quilt. Brides' quilts usually are elaborate in workmanship and sentimental in design.

Broadcloth: cotton fabric with a close, plain weave that frequently is used for quiltmaking. Broadcloth often refers to solid-color fabrics, although the same basic fabric (greige goods) can be used for both solid and printed fabrics.

Block for Bride's Quilt

B

Broderie Perse

Broderie Perse: a type of appliqué where motifs are cut from printed fabrics (such as floral designs) and appliquéd to a background.

Bunk Bed: mattress size is 38″ x 75″.

Burn Test: using a lighted candle or match to burn a sample of fabric to determine fiber content. Wool and cotton will burn with a gray smoke and will leave an ash residue. Synthetic fibers such as polyester will burn with black smoke, might smell like burning plastic, and will leave shiny black residue along the charred edge of the fabric.

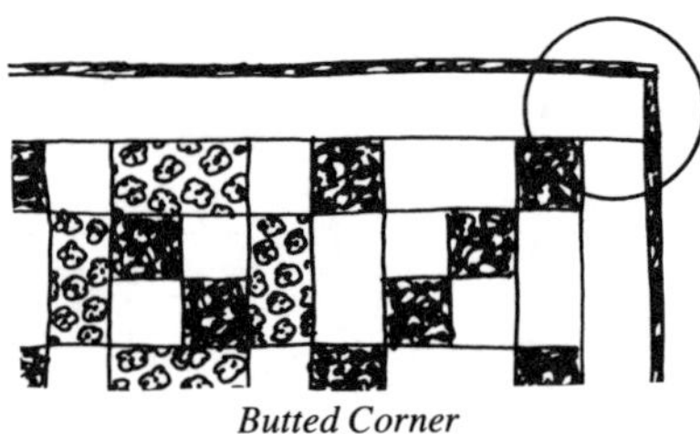
Butted Corner

Butted Corner: a corner made when one border strip is sewn past the other one at a 90° angle. Usually the side borders are added first, the ends are trimmed to be even with the quilt top, and then the top and bottom borders are added. Bindings also may have butted corners.

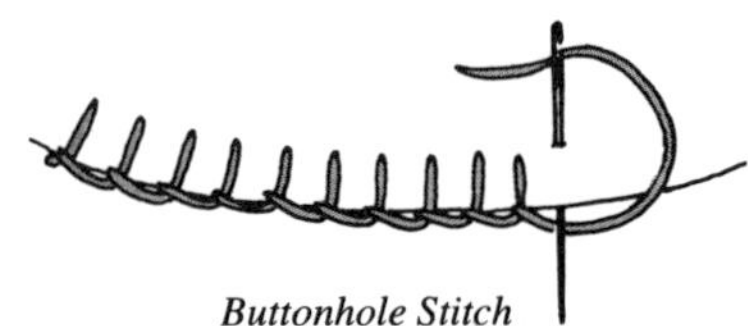
Buttonhole Stitch

Buttonhole Stitch: an embroidery stitch used for embellishing the edges of appliqué patches and for adding details on Crazy quilts or picture quilts.

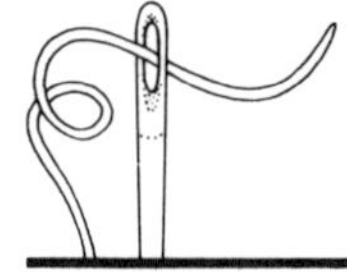

Cable Quilting

Cable Quilting: designs that resemble twisted or intertwining cords similar to that of rope.

Calico: medium-weight fabric of plain weave that is printed in a small, closely repeating design. The name

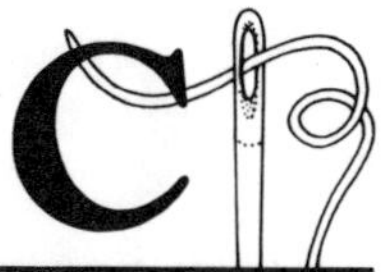

calico comes from Calicut, India, where cotton wood-block prints have been made for hundreds of years.

California King: mattress size is 72″ x 84″.

Callus: toughened skin on the finger that is pricked when hand quilting. Until a callus is developed, quilters may want to sew for short periods of time. The ouch can be soothed with various ointments or by washing dishes by hand.

Candy-Stripe Binding: a variation of patchwork binding that resembles the twirling bands of a candy cane. After piecing a parallelogram from narrow strips of fabric (often cut 1½″ wide and sewn with a 1″ "stairstep" between strips), press the pieced "fabric" with allowances to one side. Straighten the edge as shown and cut strips in the desired width. Join strips as necessary and bind the quilt, being careful not to stretch the bias edges.

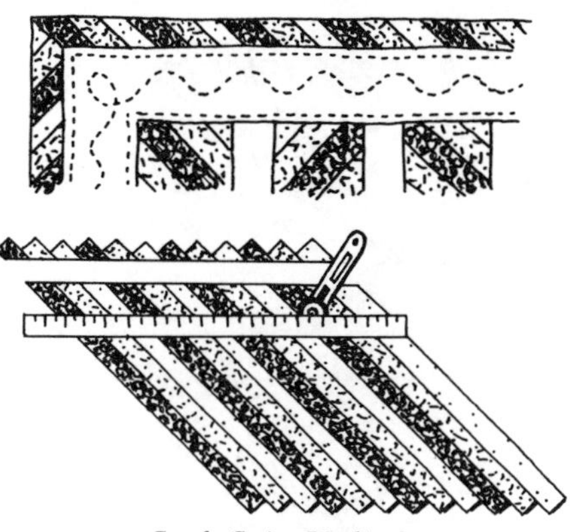

Candy-Stripe Binding

Cathedral Window: a novelty technique for making pillows and bedcovers where fabric (usually muslin) is sewn and folded in such a way that calico "windows" can be inserted. Batting, lining, and quilting are not required for cathedral window bedcovers.

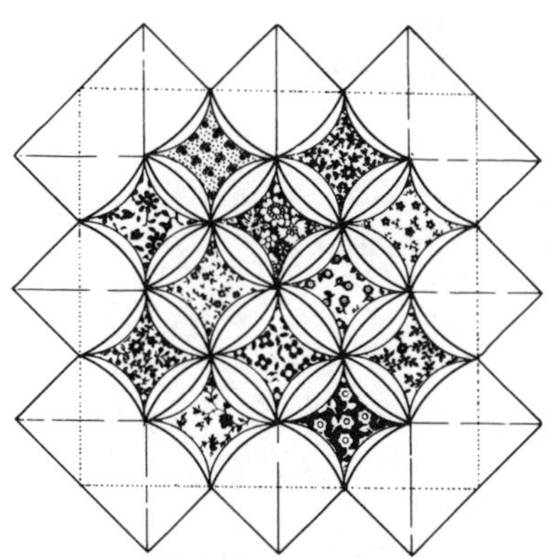

Cathedral Window Segment With 12 Windows

Celtic Designs: appliqué motifs of Irish origin made from narrow, intertwining bias strips.

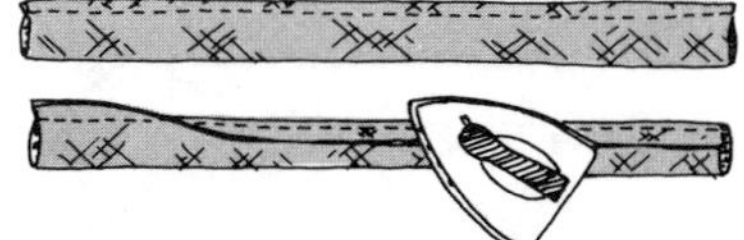

Example of Celtic Design

Chain Piecing: a technique of machine sewing where pairs of patches or

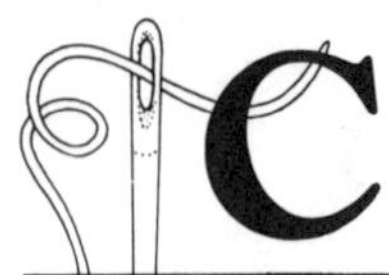

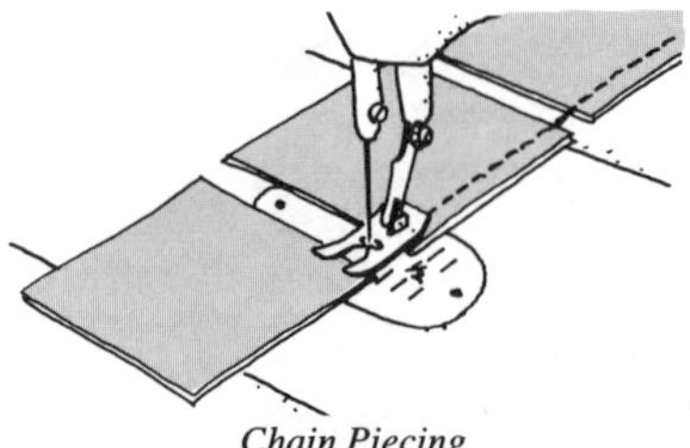

Chain Piecing

units are sewn one after the other without lifting the presser foot or clipping threads between patches. Threads connecting the patches are cut later to separate the units.

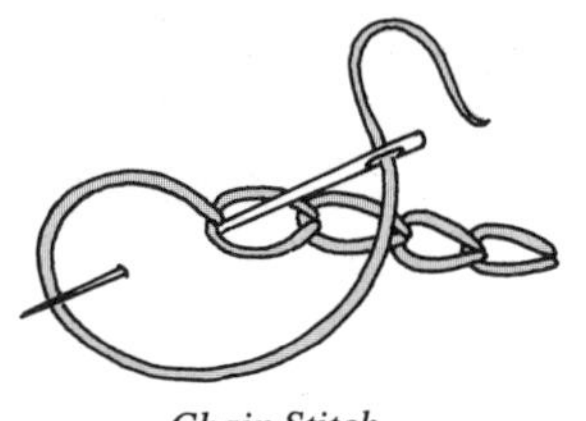

Chain Stitch

Chain Stitch: an embroidery stitch used for embellishments and inscriptions.

Challenge Quilts: quilts made from a selected group of fabrics (often with other fabrics added at the individual maker's choosing) to explore the variety of possible combinations. The making of challenge quilts is an activity that is popular with quilt groups.

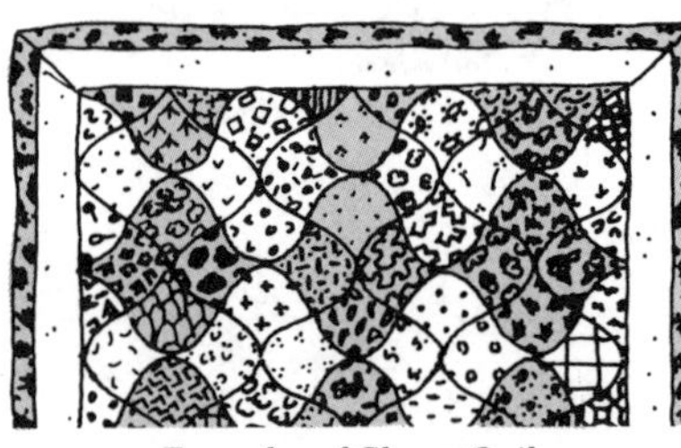

Examples of Charm Quilts

Charm Quilts: those made from a single template (such as a triangle, hexagon, or tumbler shape) and scraps of fabric with no two patches cut from the same fabric. Many quiltmakers enjoy trading small pieces of fabric to collect as many different ones as possible with which to make a charm quilt.

Cheater Cloth: a slang term referring to fabric that has been printed with patchwork designs.

Chintz: a cotton fabric with a glaze finish. Chintz is more dense than unglazed fabric and, therefore, more difficult to hand quilt. Its shine gives added highlights to quilting, especially when the fabric is a solid color. The glazing may wash or wear off in time.

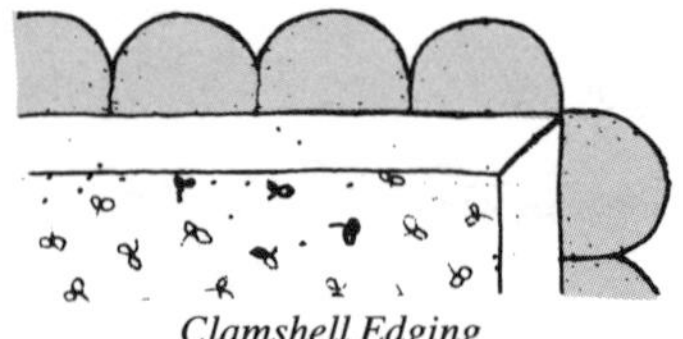

Clamshell Edging

Clamshell Edging: a novelty edging made from curved pockets that are sewn side by side or overlapping.

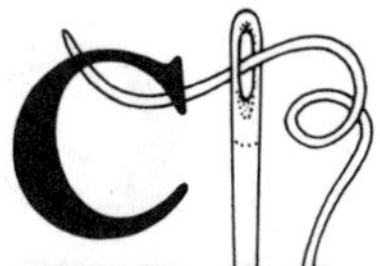

Quilts with clamshell edging do not require binding because the clamshells are sewn between the turned-under edges of the quilt top and the lining.

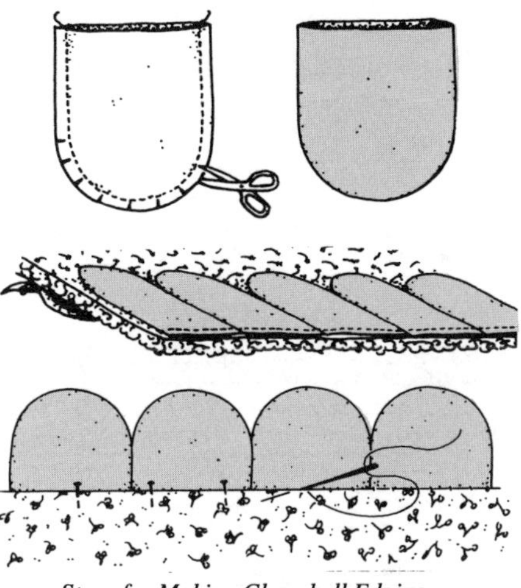
Steps for Making Clamshell Edging

Cleaning Fluid: a handy solvent to use when it is necessary to spot-clean a quilt. Cleaning fluid will easily remove sticky residue left by masking tape that was used to guide quilting lines. Test cleaning fluid on a scrap of the fabric used in the quilt before using it on the quilt itself.

Clips in Turn-Under Allowances: cuts made in the turn-under allowance, especially on indentations or concave curves, to let the allowance lie flat when it is folded under. Straight edges and convex curves rarely need clips. Indentations are clipped to within a thread of the marked line; concave curves are clipped as needed (sometimes halfway into the allowance, sometimes nearly to the marked line).

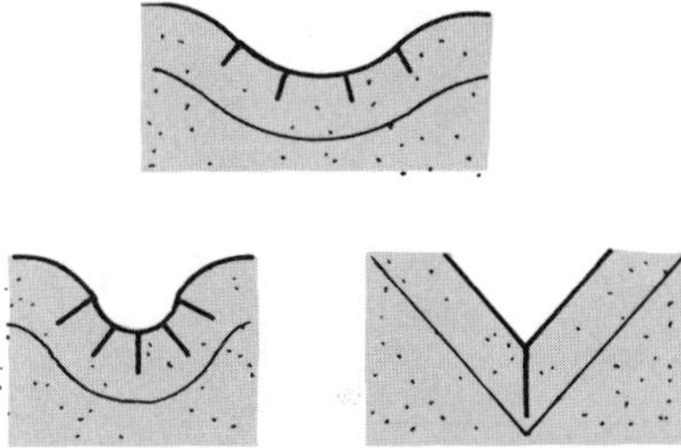
Clips in Turn-Under Allowances

Color Loss: see Bleeding, Crocking, and Light Fading.

Color Wheel: hues arranged in a circle in such a way that the colors blend in sequence like a rainbow. A basic 12-step color wheel arrangement is blue, blue/green, green, yellow/green, yellow, yellow/orange, orange, red/orange, red, red/purple, purple, and blue/purple. Many quiltmakers enjoy using a color wheel to explore color theory and fabric selection.

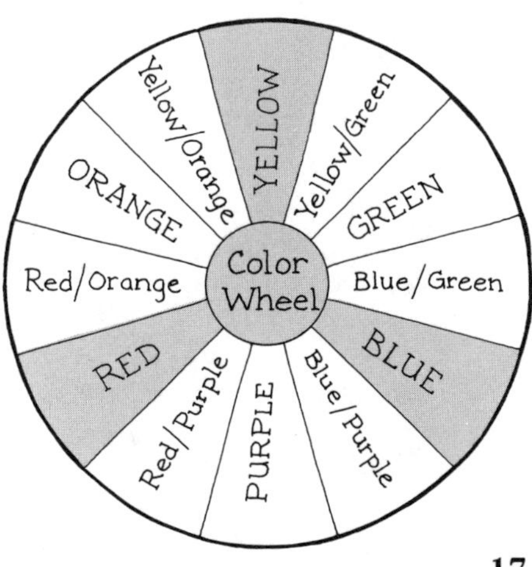

Colorfast: a term used to indicate that dye will not run when the fabric is wet.

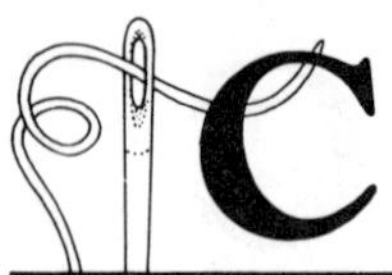

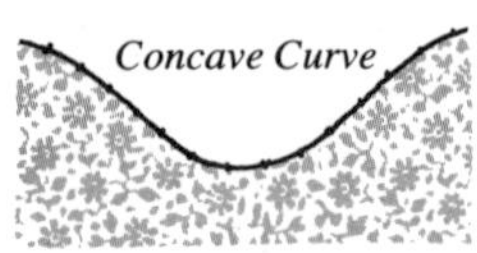

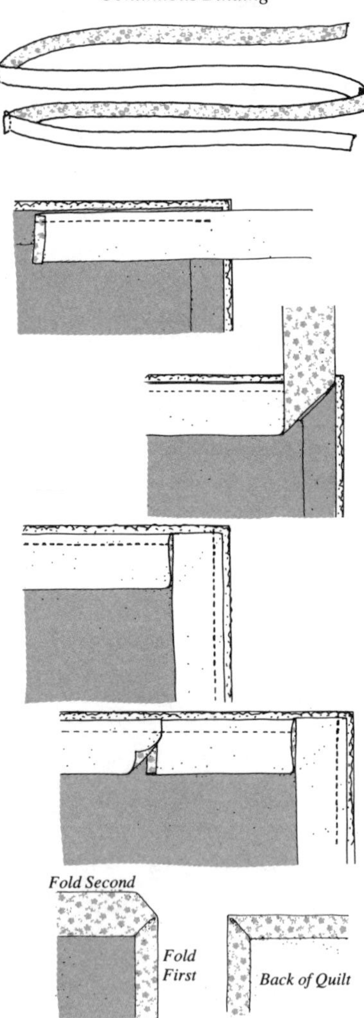

Comforter: a thick, puffy quilt that is usually tied or machine quilted rather than hand quilted. The term also can apply to quilts, smaller than bed size, to be used for naps and as lap warmers.

Concave Curve: a curve that dips in like a valley or the inside of the letter "U."

Contemporary Quilts: a term used to mean quilts that are made in the present, as opposed to those made in a past era. The term also is used in reference to quilts of new, original design, as contrasted to "traditional" quilts made from an existing pattern. Often a "contemporary" design is non-repeating, whereas a "traditional" quilt makes use of repeating blocks. There is no universal agreement on this term.

Continuous Binding: a method of finishing the edges of the quilt with one long strip of binding that is pieced from shorter lengths. Referring to the figures, pin binding on one front edge of the quilt. Machine stitch to the end of the seam line (not to the edge of the quilt); backstitch and remove the quilt from under the needle. Fold the binding strip to make a diagonal pleat; put the quilt back under the needle and sew from the edge of quilt to the end of the seam line. Backstitch, remove quilt, and fold the strip as before. Continue this process to bind all four edges of the quilt. Turn binding to the back side and fold under the allowance to cover the machine stitching. Blindstitch the fold. At corners, fold binding in the sequence shown.

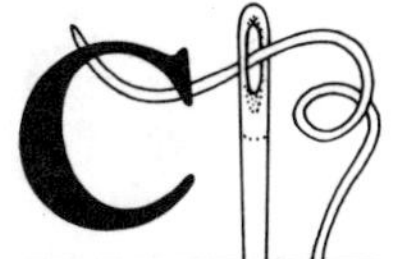

Continous-Line Machine Quilting: a technique using unbroken design lines that can be stitched with minimal stopping and starting. See Machine Quilting.

Examples of Continuous-Line Machine Quilting

Contrast: variance in light and dark fabric colors or size/type of prints to allow patches to be distinct.

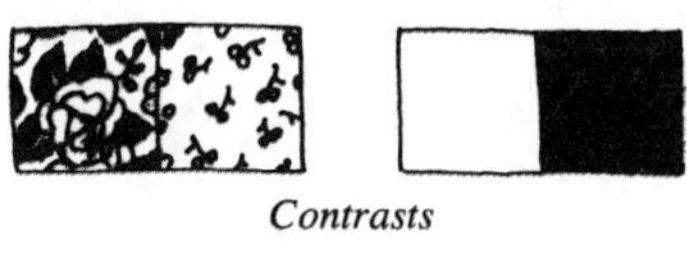

Contrasts

Convex Curve: a curve such as that of a rainbow or the outside of the letter "O."

Convex Curve

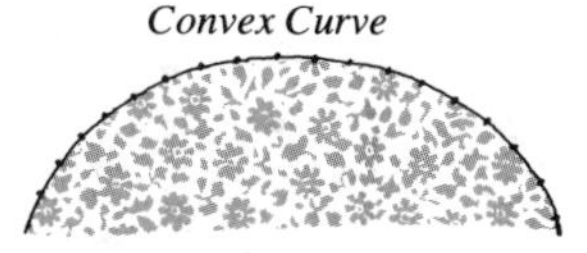

Corded Edging: the sewing of fabric-covered cording between the turned-under edges of the quilt top and lining in place of binding. Cording also can be used with binding by sewing it just inside the binding on the front of the quilt.

Corner Triangles: patches (which usually are large) that are sewn on to square up a quilt top made from blocks that are joined in diagonal rows. Outer edges usually should be straight grain.

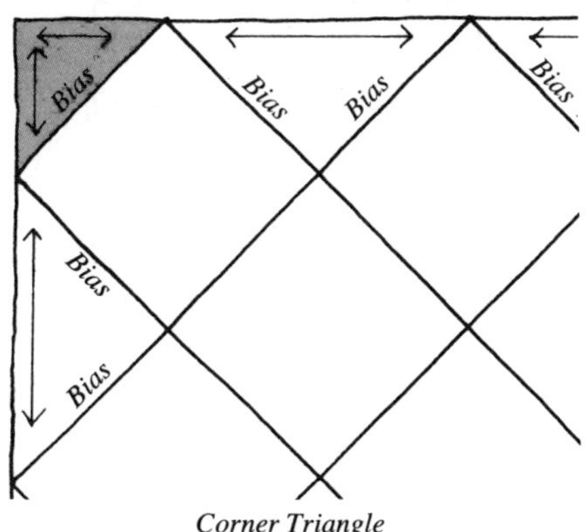

Corner Triangle
Arrows Indicate Grain Lines

Cotton Batting: that which is made from cotton fiber. (There is also a cotton/polyester blend batting.) Most cotton batting is not designed for beginning hand quilters because it requires close quilting and is not as easy to quilt through as polyester batting. Cotton batting produces a quilt that is flatter than one with polyester batting. A quilt that is made with cotton batting may shrink when it is washed.

Cotton Fabric: the most suitable fabric to use for appliqué and piecing be-

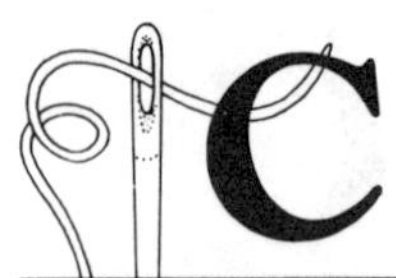

Example of a Counterchange Pattern

Coverlet With a Dust Ruffle

Crazy Quilting

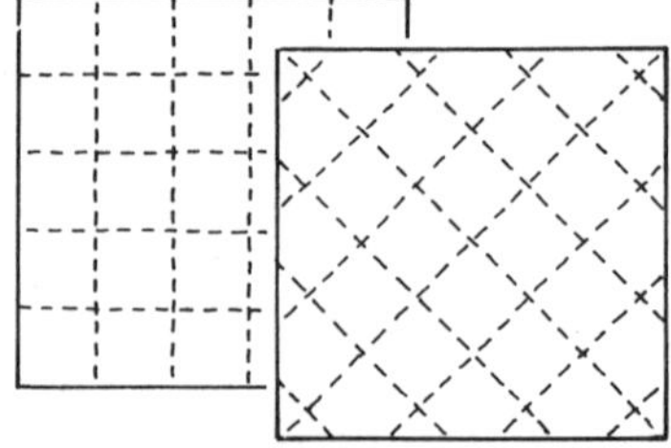
Cross-Hatching

cause of its stability and its ability to retain a crisp crease. Cotton fabric is available in nearly any solid color and a wide variety of prints. Most quiltmakers collect fabric to build an extensive palette of material.

Counterchange Patterns: quilt designs that use two contrasting fabrics. Alternate blocks have the two fabrics reversed. Counterchange quilts can be very graphic if the fabrics have high contrast.

Coverlet: a quilt made to cover the top of a bed and the sides of the mattress but not made large enough to drop to the floor. Coverlets often are used with dust ruffles.

Crazy Quilt: fancy patchwork incorporating silk, velvet, and embroidery popular in the late-19th century and among some quiltmakers today. Crazy quilts are constructed on a muslin foundation fabric and usually do not include batting although they may have a lining.

Crib: mattress size is 28″ x 52″.

Crocking: the rubbing off of fabric dye. If you discover that your fingers take on the color of fabric you are piecing or quilting, the dye is crocking. Washing or rinsing fabric before cutting and sewing will often remove excess dye so that it does not crock. Also see Bleeding.

Cross-Hatching: parallel lines of quilting that run in two directions, forming

either a grid of squares or a grid of diamonds. Cross-hatching is sometimes used in the background of appliqué quilts or to set off quilting motifs.

Cross Stitch: a decorative embroidery stitch that is especially good for signatures and inscriptions on quilts. It can be done by eye (without marking) or can be worked over waste canvas using a charted design.

Cross-Stitch Quilts: those made with cross-stitch embroidery as the primary design. Such quilts often are made from printed blocks or panels. Before beginning a quilt project with commercially printed markings, check to be sure the markings can be removed or be certain to cover them with the embroidery.

Crosswise Grain: the fabric threads that are woven from selvedge to selvedge, called weft or filling threads. Crosswise grain has some stretch, but not as much as bias.

Curved Seams: lines of stitching joining patches that have rounded edges. Curved seams usually require clips in the seam allowances of the concave curve to allow easier sewing. Careful pinning and sewing are needed for accuracy; marked notches will help in matching seam lines.

Cut-As-You-Go Appliqué: a technique where the design is marked on fabric but not cut out. This marked fabric is basted to the background fabric, then the top fabric is trimmed 3⁄16″ outside the marked line for a few inches.

Cross Stitch

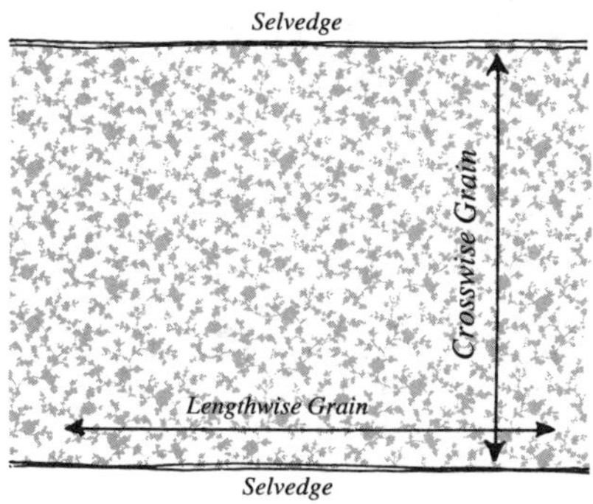

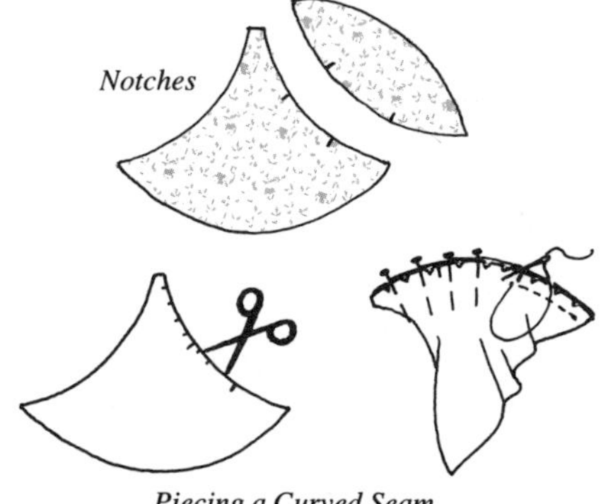

Piecing a Curved Seam

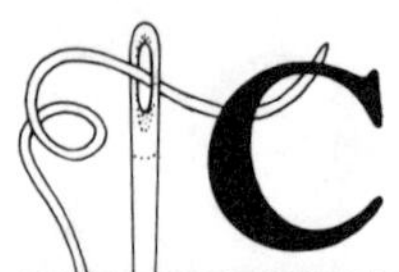

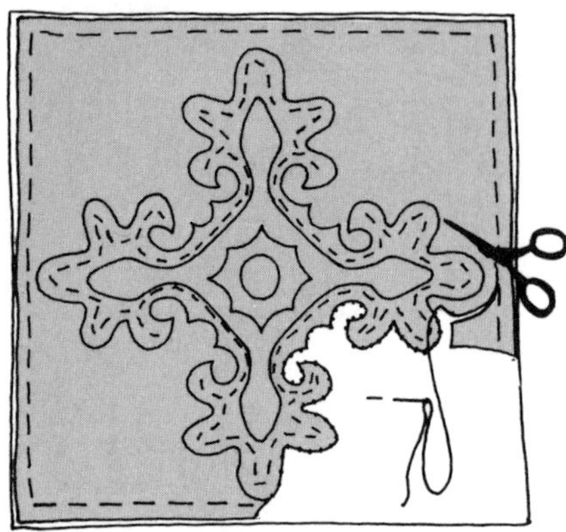

Cut-As-You-Go Appliqué

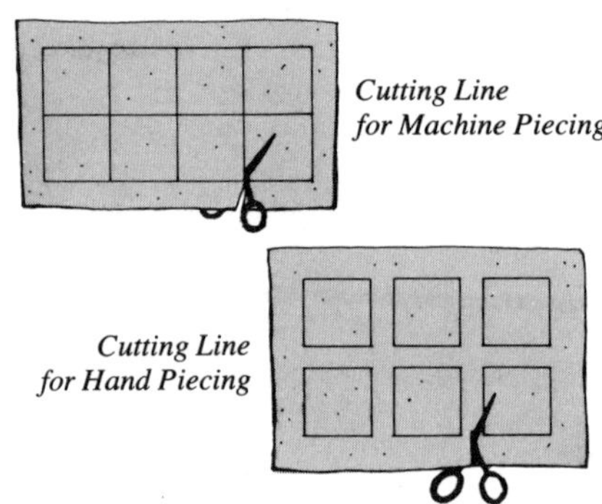

Cutting Line for Machine Piecing

Cutting Line for Hand Piecing

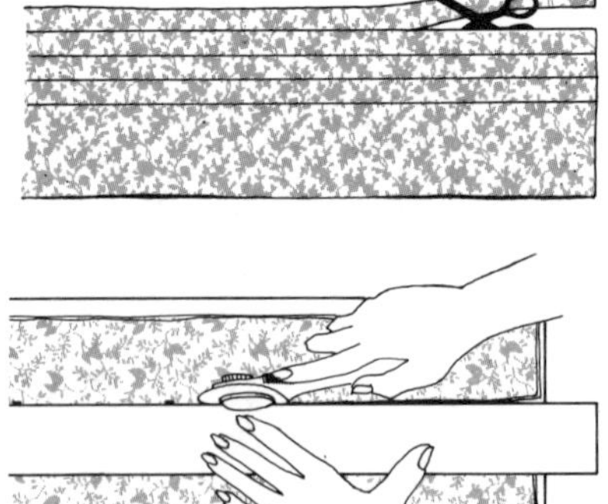

Cutting Strips

The allowance is turned under and blindstitched for a short distance, then another inch or so is trimmed. The stitching and trimming are alternated as the work progresses.

Cutter Quilts: a term given to old quilts that are cut up to make stuffed animals, garments, and household accessories. Many quiltmakers strongly oppose the cutting up of old quilts because they are irreplaceable antiques.

Cutting Line: the line on which patches are cut out. Patches to be machine pieced are cut on marked lines because templates for machine piecing include the seam allowance. Cutting lines for hand-pieced patches are determined "by eye" approximately ¼″ from the marked seam lines because templates for hand piecing do not include seam allowances.

Cutting Mat: a special protective surface on which a rotary cutter can be used safely.

Cutting Strips: the preferred method of "making" plain border strips and straight-grain binding (as opposed to tearing them). Cut the strips with scissors after marking lines, or use a rotary cutter, cutting mat, and see-through template (which can also serve as a ruler).

Cyanotype Printing: a method of developing photographs on fabric using a negative and cotton material that has been coated with light-sensitive chemicals. The resulting image is always blue.

Decorative Stitches: embroidery stitches used to accent appliqué designs, sign a name or inscription, outline seams on a Crazy quilt, or otherwise embellish a design.

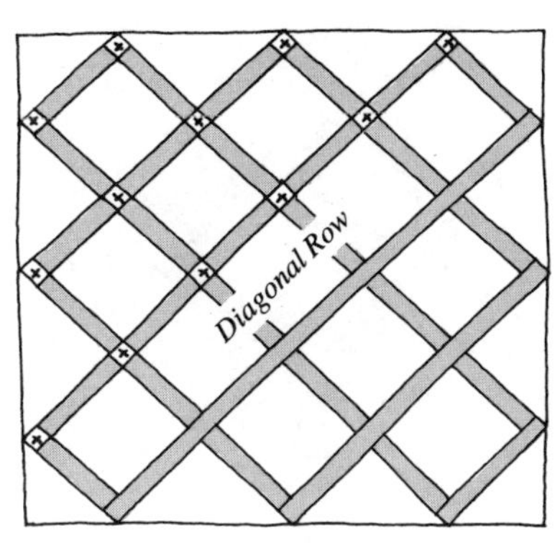

x = Setting Square
= Sashing

Diagonal Row: a row of blocks, with or without sashing, that crosses the quilt at a 45° angle. If setting squares are not used, sashing for diagonal rows will be cut in several different lengths to accommodate the varying number of blocks in the rows. If setting squares are used, all sashes will be identical.

Double Bed: mattress size is 54″ x 75″. Double beds also are called full size.

Double Binding: binding that finishes with a double layer of fabric. Double binding is cut four times the finished width plus two seam allowances (often about 2¼″ total). Fold binding in half lengthwise (wrong sides together), press, and sew it to the front side of the quilt with both raw edges of binding matching the edge of the quilt. When turning binding to the back, there is no need to turn under the edge. Simply blindstitch the fold so it just covers the stitching.

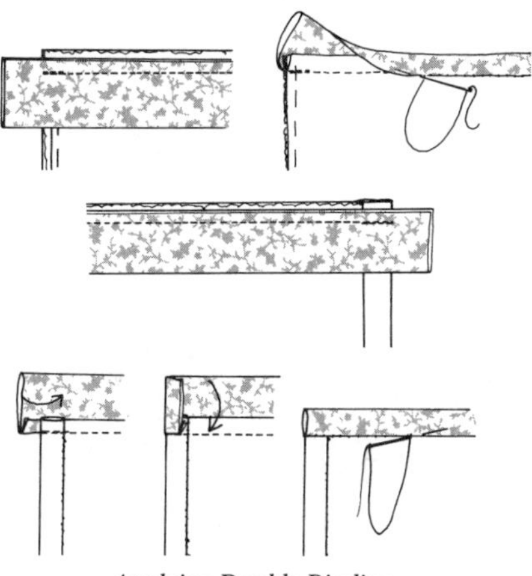

Applying Double Binding

Drafting: the drawing of an accurate pattern to be used for marking and cutting patches.

Drop: the distance from the top of a mattress to the floor or the part of a quilt that falls from the top of the mattress (whether or not it extends to the floor).

The Drop of a Quilt

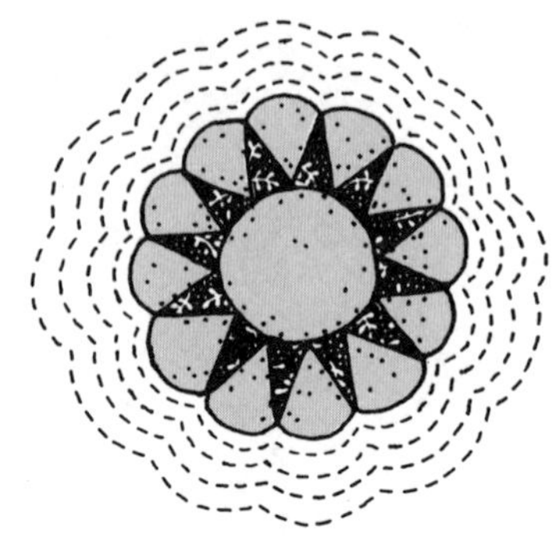

Echo Quilting

Various Kinds of Edge Finishing

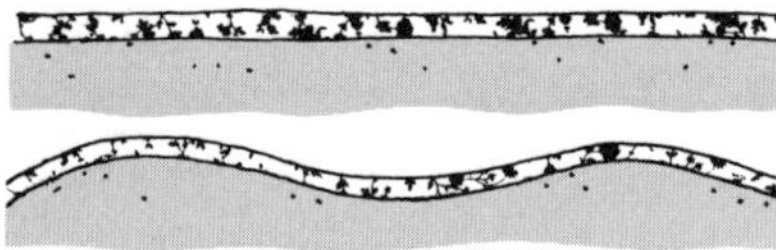

Binding, Straight or Curved Edge

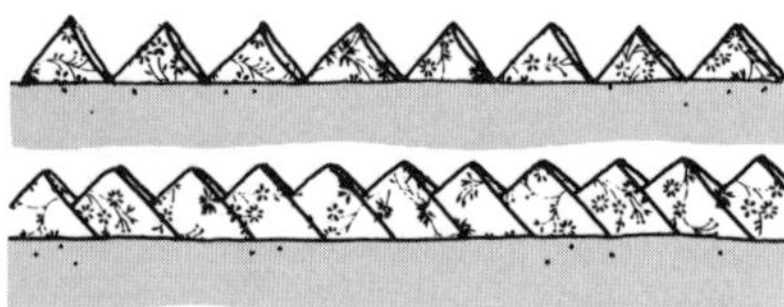

Prairie Points

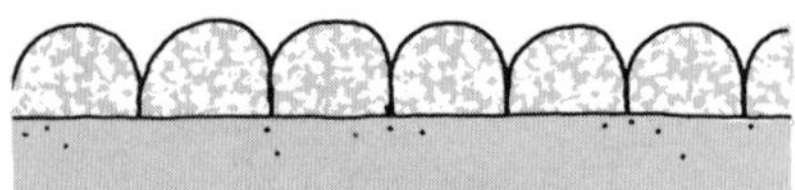

Clamshell Edging

Ruffled Edging

Easing: a technique to make unequal parts of the quilt match at seams by evenly distributing the fullness of one segment across the edge of the other segment. Easing is used to control unevenness and make the finished quilt lie (or hang) flat and smooth. When pinning two sections with one of them to be eased, use a lot of pins to evenly space the extra fullness. Often the edges of the quilt will be a bit too long and will require easing onto the border. Placing the fuller edge next to the feed dogs and stretching the shorter edge on top as it is sewn helps avoid any tucks.

Echo Quilting: lines of quilting that outline appliqué shapes (often on Hawaiian quilts) in concentric rings or shapes. Lines of echo quilting usually are about ½″ apart and often are judged by eye without marking.

Edge Finishing: any of several techniques that encase or embellish the perimeter of the quilt. Binding is the most common edge finish; other techniques include adding prairie points, ruffles, clamshells, or corded edging. As the edges are being finished, the batting should be secured with sewing so that it does not shift. The edges usually are finished after the quilting or tying is complete.

Edge Triangles: companion patches to corner triangles, these are used to fill in the triangular gaps at the edges of a quilt that has diagonally set blocks.

Embroidery Floss: six-strand thread

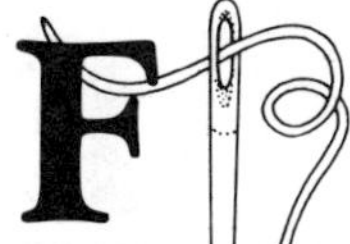

used for decorative embroidery and for tying quilts. Cotton floss comes in hundreds of colors; rayon and silk floss also are available, but in limited colors.

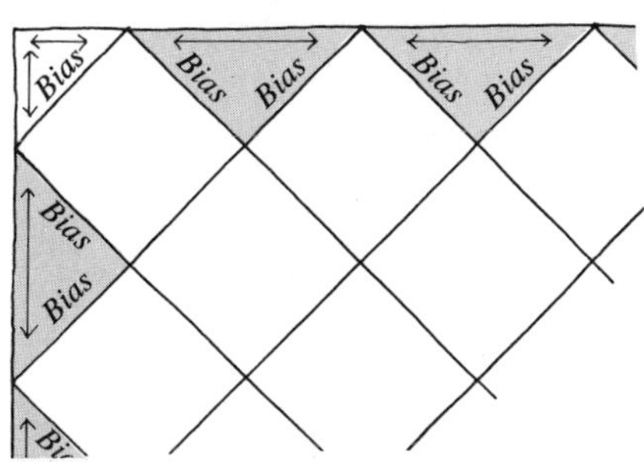

Edge Triangles
Arrows Indicate Grain Lines

English Piecing: a technique for piecing in which medium-weight paper is cut to the exact size of a finished patch and fabric is basted over the paper. After patches are basted, they are placed right sides together and joined with tiny overcast stitches. The basting is taken out and the papers are removed. This technique is often used for pieced patterns that would otherwise require set-in patches, such as six- and eight-pointed star designs made from diamonds. Many quilts made with English piecing have hexagon-shaped patches that form a design called Grandmother's Flower Garden.

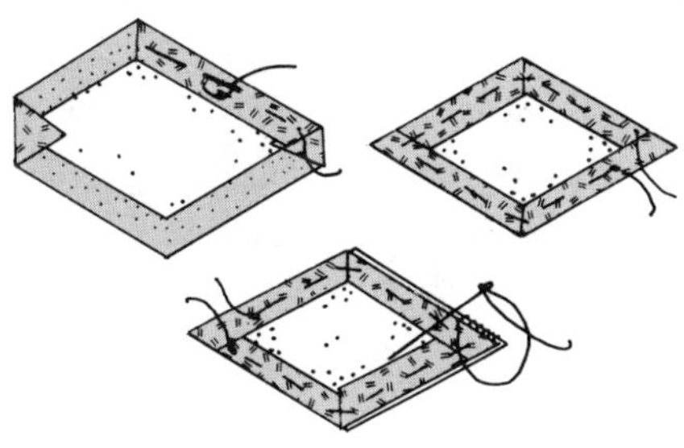

English Piecing

Even-Feed Foot: see Walking Foot.

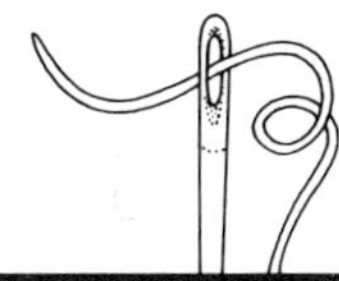

Fabric: for quiltmaking, the material that is favored is usually 100 percent cotton of medium weight. The threads should be woven closely enough so that small quilting stitches will not fall between the threads. Dyes should be colorfast, and the fabric should not have a heavy or stiff finish if it will be hand quilted. Quiltmakers certainly are not limited to cotton fabrics; every imaginable kind of textile has been used to make quilts. However, quilts to be washed should be made of washable fabric.

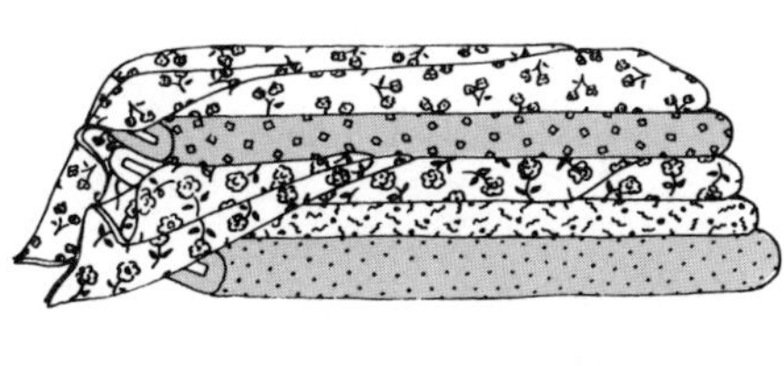

F

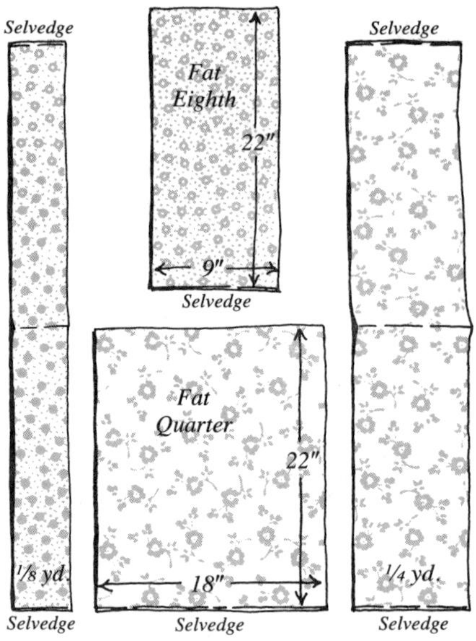

Fabric Crayons or Markers: implements for drawing on material to be sewn into a quilt. Some of these markers require the use of an iron to set the color; others do not. Using crayons or markers is a good way to introduce children and adults to quiltmaking, and it can be an excellent medium for making a friendship quilt.

Fat Batting: extra-thick batting used for tied comforters and, occasionally, for machine-quilted quilts. Fat batting does not allow hand quilters to achieve stitches as small as those possible with thinner batting of light or medium weight.

Fat Eighth: a piece of fabric cut half width (approximately 22″) by 9″. The total number of square inches is the same as that of ⅛ yard of fabric.

Fat Quarter: a piece of fabric cut half width (approximately 22″) by 18″. The total number of square inches is the same as that of ¼ yard of fabric. The advantage of "fat" pieces of fabric is that larger patches can sometimes be cut from them than from the corresponding amount of fabric that is cut full width.

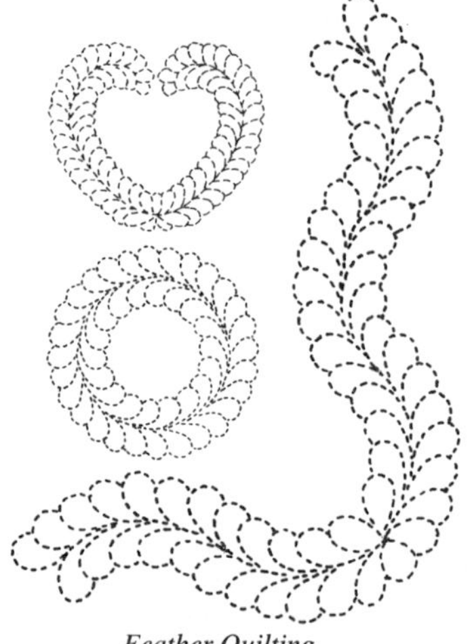

Feather Quilting

Feather Quilting: a favorite design motif, with many variations, that is used in blocks, background, and borders. Individual rounded feathers extend from a center spine that is usually curved but also can be straight.

Feather Stitch

Feather Stitch: a decorative embroidery stitch used for outlining Crazy-

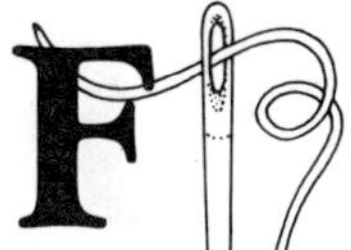

quilt patches or appliqué.

Feed: the process of putting patches under the needle and presser foot of a sewing machine. The patches are guided and moved along by rows of metal teeth called feed dogs.

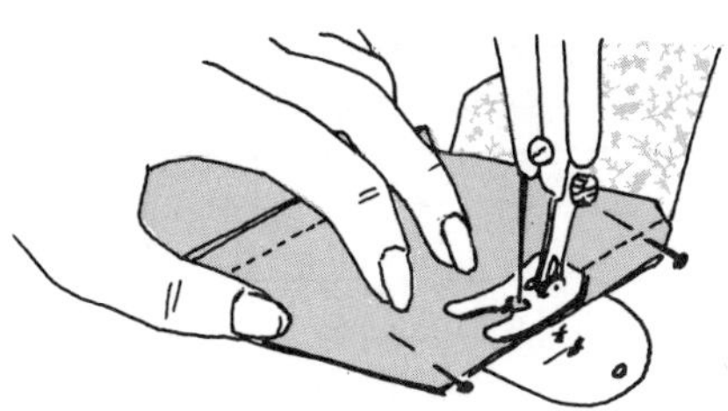
Feeding Patches

Feed Dogs: the metal teeth that guide and move fabric under the needle of the sewing machine. Feed dogs are lowered (disengaged) for free-motion quilting and free-form appliqué.

Feed Dogs

Feed Sacks: cloth bags made of cotton, in which grain and flour were (and still are) packaged, that were used to make quilts in the 1930s and 1940s during a time of economic hardship.

Feed Sacks

Fiber Content: the composition of a fabric, which is usually given in percentages. Natural fibers are cotton, wool, silk, and linen; man-made fibers include nylon, polyester, and acrylic. Rayon is man-made from processed cellulose. Material used for quilts is usually 100 percent cotton, but many quilters also use blends of cotton and polyester or other fibers.

Fiber Migration: see Bearding.

Fiberfill: polyester stuffing used to fill pillows and stuffed toys and to use in trapunto.

Finger Press: to use your fingers to flatten seam allowances or fold guidelines in fabric (for appliqué, for instance). Cotton fabric is more easily and effectively finger pressed than are

Finger Pressing

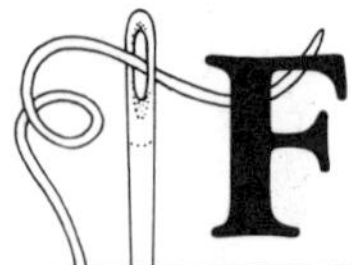

F

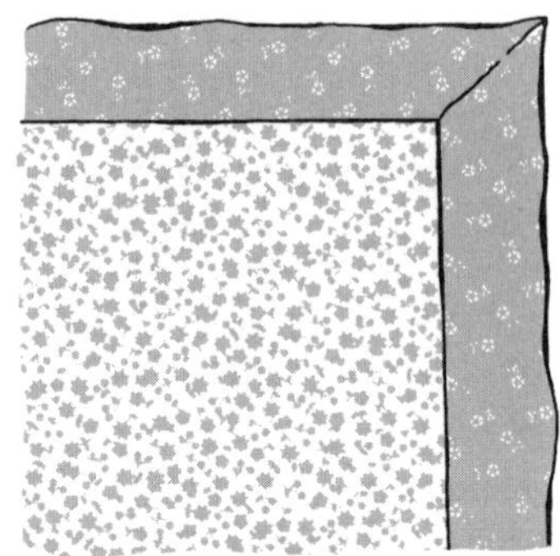

Flaring Borders

Floating Blocks

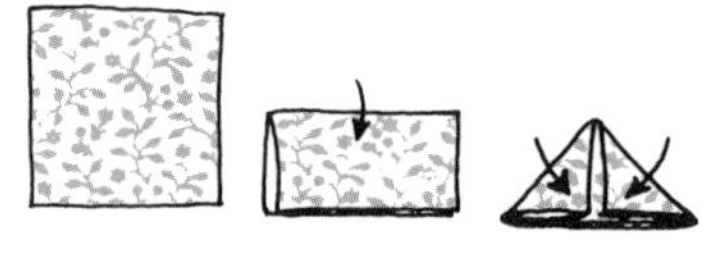

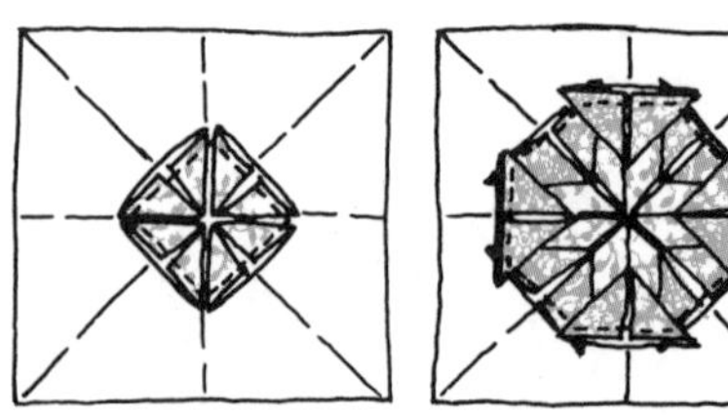

Folded-Star Construction

other fibers. Finger pressing has two advantages: It can be done anywhere without the need for an iron, and it will press out with no permanent creases.

Flannel Board: a handy work surface for mounting patches (with or without pins) to see how they look before sewing them together. Any kind of cardboard or wood can be covered with fuzzy flannel, or a piece of flannel fabric can be stapled to a wall in your sewing room.

Flannel Fabric: an alternate filler (in place of batting) that will produce a very flat quilt with no loft. Whether it is purchased as yardage or as a bed sheet, flannel must be washed and dried before it is used in a quilt, because it can shrink considerably.

Flaring: extra fullness or rippling of borders caused by borders being cut too long or by borders not being quilted sufficiently.

Floating Blocks: the effect created when sashing matches the block background. For example, if Pine Tree blocks are set with sashes that match the background fabric, the sashes will blend with that fabric and allow the trees to appear unbordered, as if they are floating.

Folded Star: a novelty technique used to make quilt blocks, potholders, pillows, and other items in which squares of fabric are folded and stitched to a fabric base. The squares are layered in sequence to make a star design.

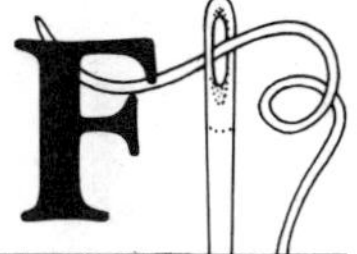

Foundation Fabric: a piece of material used as a base on which patches are sewn for some types of Log Cabin and Crazy quilt blocks. Because foundation fabrics do not show in the finished quilt, many quiltmakers use muslin or their "ugly" fabric as the foundation.

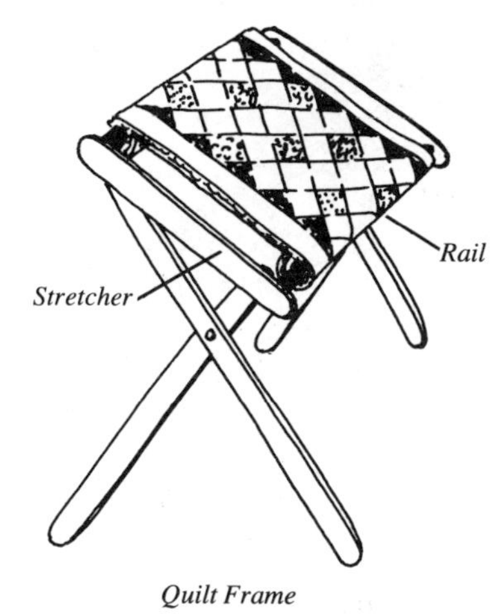

Quilt Frame

Frame: (1) a wood (or plastic) piece of furniture that stretches and holds the quilt so it can be quilted. Many quilting frames are large enough for six or more people to quilt at one time, making them ideal for group quilts or "quilting bees." These frames have two long rails on which the quilt is rolled, two side stretchers, and legs to position the quilt at a comfortable height for quilting. Many different styles and sizes of quilting frames are available.

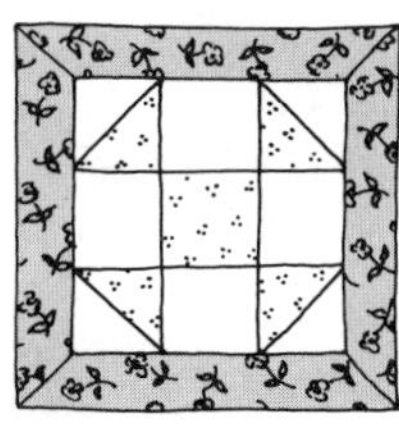

Frame: (2) a border sewn to all sides of a block as the block is made.

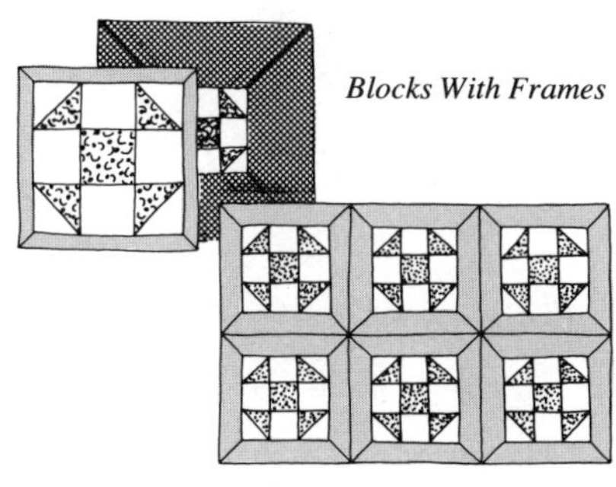

Blocks With Frames

Frame Width: (see 2 above) dimensions that can vary from narrow to wide, perhaps to be even wider than the block (especially if the block is small). The sizes of the block patches often can guide in planning frame width. If framed blocks are joined side by side and if frames are made from only one fabric, the result will be double-frame-width stripping between blocks.

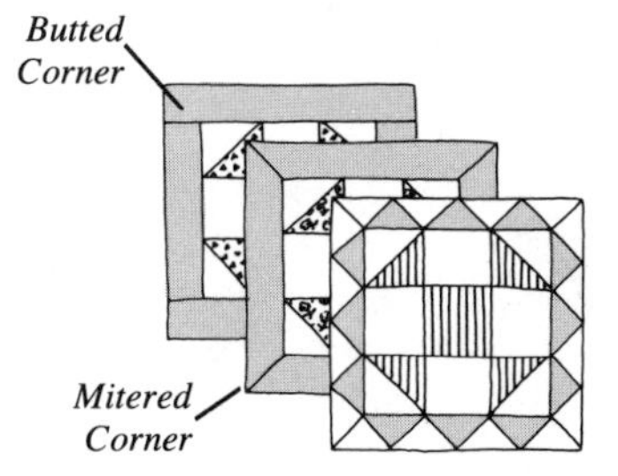

Framing Strips: rectangular patches of fabric sewn to block edges to make a frame. Corners are usually either mitered or butted, or the framing strips themselves can be pieced. For best accuracy, framing strips should be cut using templates.

Landscape Made With Free-Form Appliqué

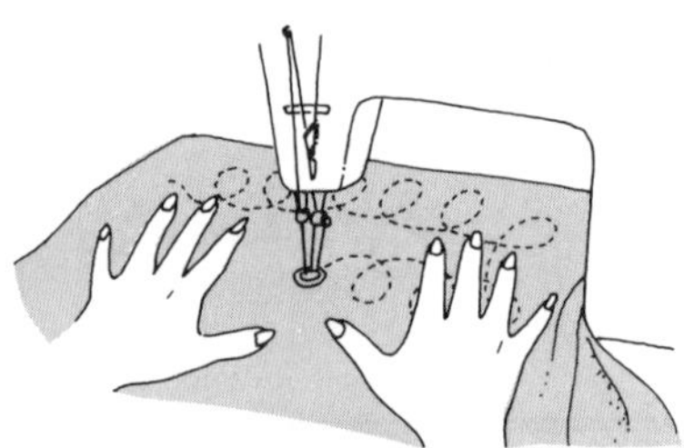

Free-Motion Quilting

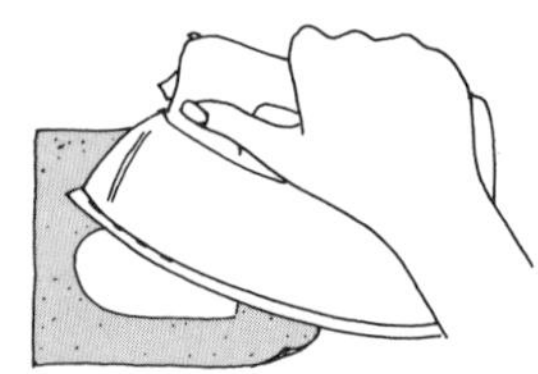

Freezer-Paper Pressed Shiny Side Down

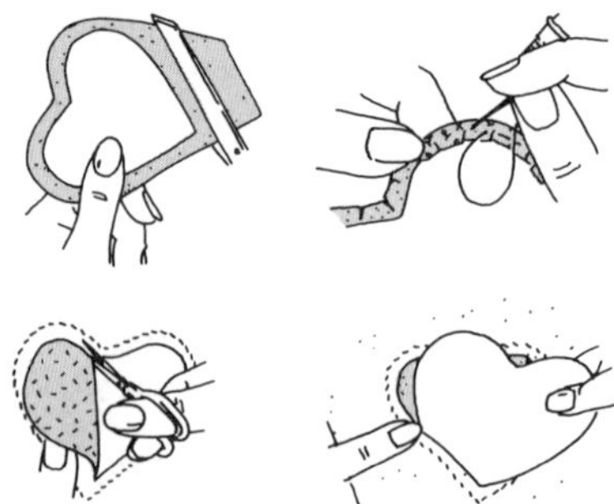

Free-Form Appliqué: an appliqué technique in which there is no marked turn-under line and no basting. The allowance is turned under by eye, with the result that the finished shape will not be exactly predictable. This method is used for such patches as the rolling hills of a landscape.

Free-Motion Quilting: machine quilting for which the feed dogs are lowered and the quilt is maneuvered in any direction (without turning it) under a darning foot, which replaces the regular presser foot.

Freedom Quilt: in the 19th century, a quilt made for a young man as he approached his age of majority. Today, a quilt made for anyone (male or female) who is about to set out on his or her own, whether that means going away to college or getting an apartment.

Freezer-Paper Appliqué: a popular technique (with two variations) where freezer paper (available at the grocery store for packaging food to be frozen) is cut to the exact size of the finished appliqué patch, either with the shiny (waxy) side up or with the shiny side down. If the shiny side is cut as the right side of the patch, it is pressed shiny side down on the wrong side of fabric. The fabric is then cut to allow 3/16″-1/4″ allowance outside the paper, the fabric is folded and basted around the paper, and the patch is appliquéd in place. After the background is cut away behind the appliqué, the basting and paper are removed. If the shiny side is the wrong side of the patch, the fabric

is cut about ¼″ larger than the paper. The paper is placed in the center of the fabric patch and the tip of an iron is used to press the allowance to the paper. (The iron should not be placed directly over the shiny part of the paper.) The patch is then placed on the background, pressed in place, and appliquéd. After the background is cut away behind the appliqué, the paper is removed. Freezer-paper techniques are especially useful with wiggly fabric such as silk.

Freezer-Paper Pressed Shiny Side Up

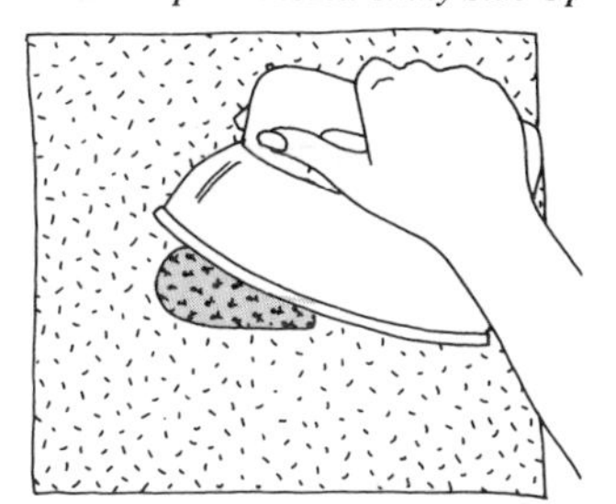

French Knot: a decorative embroidery stitch that makes tiny ball-shape knots that can dot an "i" or serve as embellishments for appliqué.

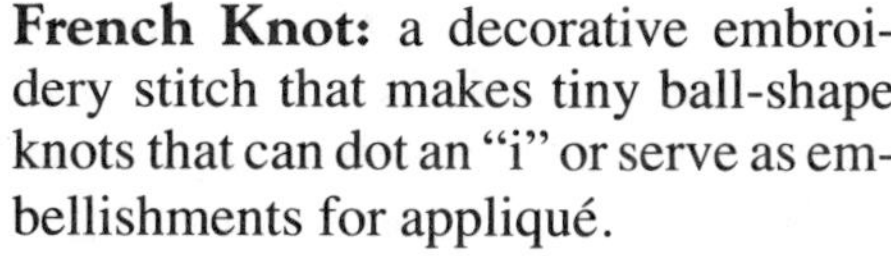

Friendship Quilts: group quilts, often made from scraps and varying patterns, that usually have signed blocks. Friendship quilts may commemorate a birthday, wedding anniversary, retirement, or some other special occasion.

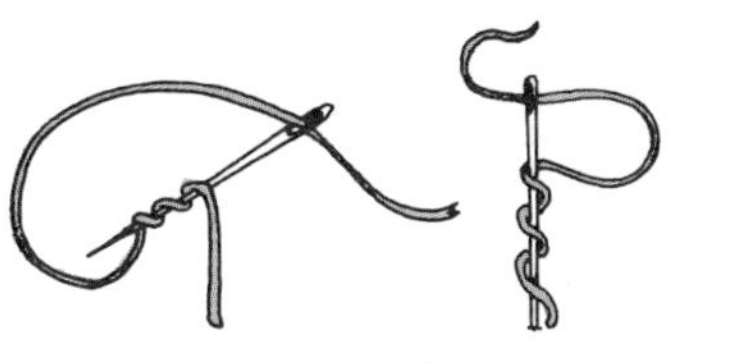

French Knot

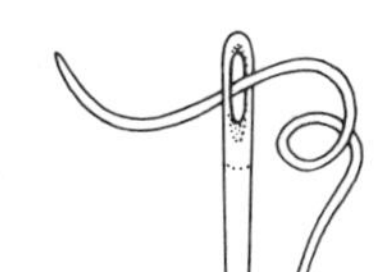

Glue Stick: easy-to-apply adhesive for temporarily holding appliqué patches in place while sewing. Purchase a glue stick intended for use with fabric, not one for use on paper.

Grain Lines: lengthwise and crosswise threads that are woven to make fabric. Grain-line placement is indicated on patterns with grain-line arrows; arrows should be placed parallel to fabric threads. Crosswise grain provides some stretch but offers only a maximum di-

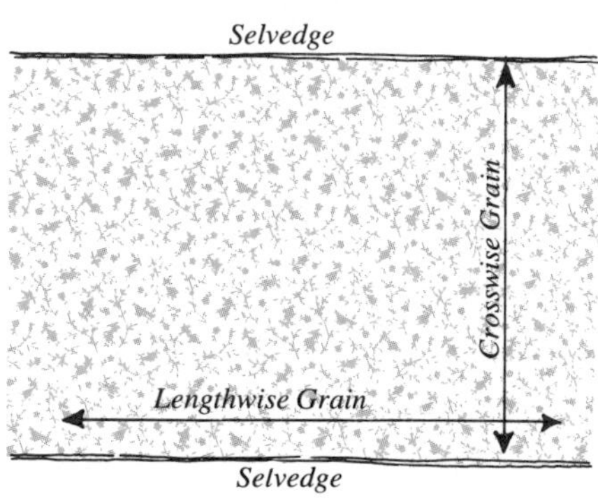

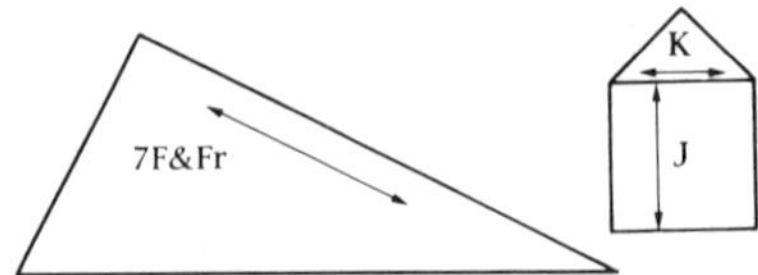

Patterns With Grain-Line Arrows

mension of about 42″ without seaming. Lengthwise grain does not stretch, and borders cut this way can be any dimension required without the necessity of seaming short pieces. Border strips can be cut on crosswise grain or lengthwise grain.

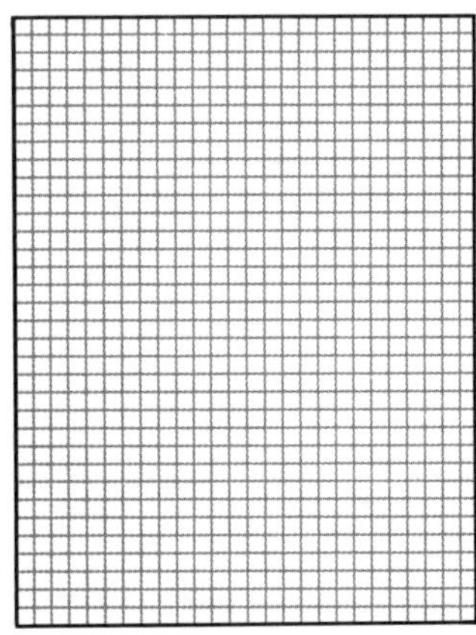
Graph Paper

Graph Paper: gridded paper that is used in planning quilts by drawing blocks with other components such as frames, setting squares, and sashing in miniature to experiment with ideas and check proportions. Graph-paper drawings can be photocopied and colored to experiment further with design. One kind of graph paper, printed with light blue lines, is especially good if drawings will be photocopied because the lines will not show in the copies. Graph paper is also excellent for use in drafting full-size patterns, which can be glued to cardboard or traced on plastic to make templates. Graph paper is available by the sheet or by the yard.

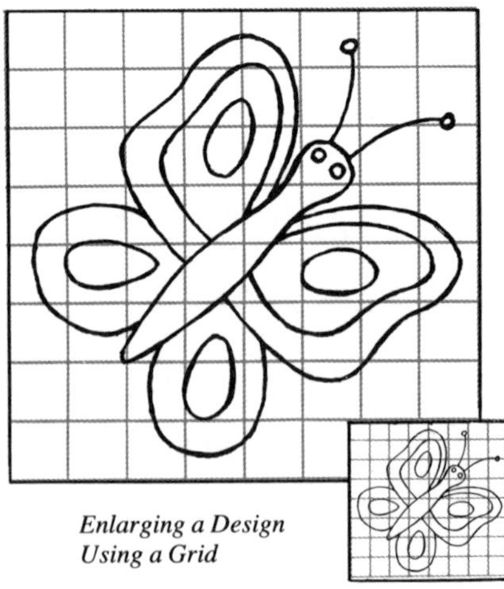
Enlarging a Design Using a Grid

Greige Goods: (pronounced "gray goods") unfinished fabric that is not yet dyed, printed, or finished with sizing. It is the raw material from which fabrics are processed.

Grid: equally spaced horizontal and vertical lines that are used when enlarging a design. Grid lines are drawn on the design to be enlarged, then a proportionately larger grid is drawn and the lines from each square of the smaller design are marked. By dividing a design with a grid this way, it is easier to be accurate in drawing the enlarged version.

Hand (of Fabric): the qualities of fabric as perceived by the way it feels. Soft fabric that is neither stiff nor flimsy is the best choice for most quilts.

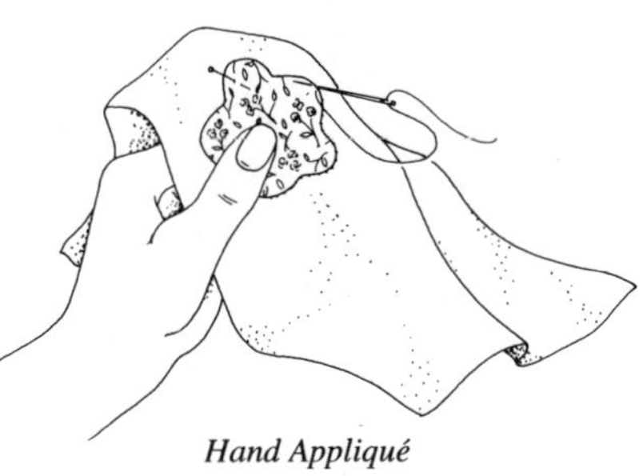

Hand Appliqué

Hand Appliqué: to apply patches with hand sewing, usually using the blind stitch, to a background fabric. Patches for hand appliqué should include turn-under allowance and usually have marked sewing lines.

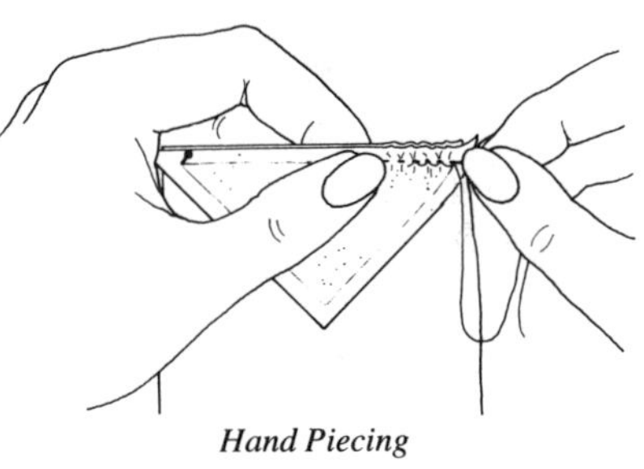

Hand Piecing

Hand Piecing: to sew patches together with a hand-held needle and a single strand of thread. Hand piecing is usually done with a running stitch and backstitches to begin and end the seam. Many quiltmakers consider hand piecing to be relaxing and precise because of its slow pace.

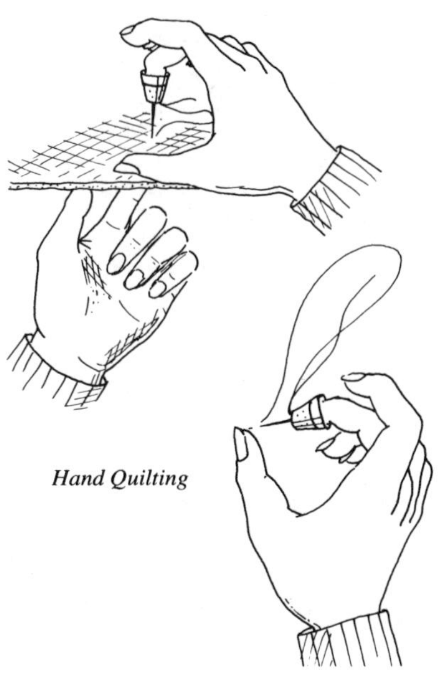

Hand Quilting

Hand Quilting: fastening together the layers of the quilt with running stitches. When a frame or hoop is used, one hand controls the needle on top of the quilt; the other hand guides the needle under the quilt. Beginning quilters might take one stitch at a time; more often quilters use a rocking motion to put several stitches on the needle before pulling it through. Because the needle is pushed with the middle finger of the sewing hand, it is important to wear a thimble on that finger to protect it. Hand quilting a quilt can (but doesn't always) take as long as or longer than making the quilt top. For faster results, the quilt can be machine quilted or tied.

Hawaiian Quilting: a style of quilt design, originating in Hawaii and now enjoyed by quilters everywhere, with

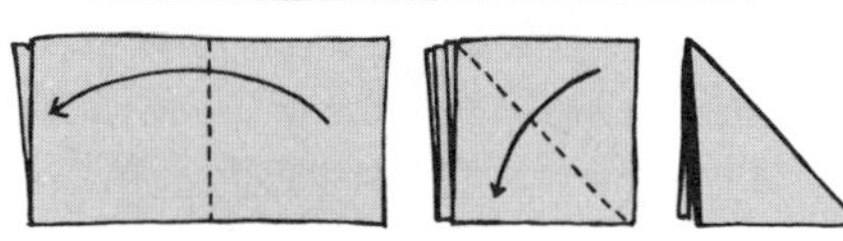

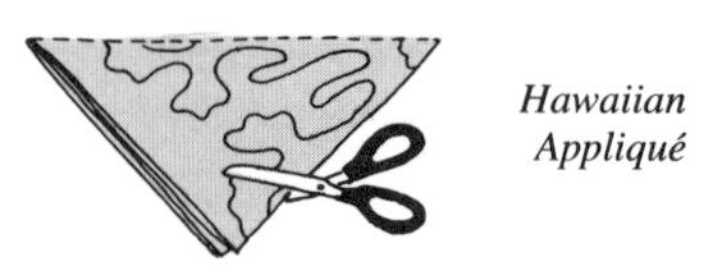

Hawaiian Appliqué

one large appliqué cut from folded fabric in the same way as paper snowflakes are cut. The appliqué is basted to the background fabric, then the allowance is turned under "by eye" without a marked line. Hawaiian quilts customarily have only two colors of fabric, both of which are solid. They are usually quilted in parallel lines of echo quilting.

Heritage Quilt Projects: programs and activities to document historic quilts in a state or region. Quilt guilds are often involved with these events.

Hmong Needlework: a distinct style of appliqué, embroidery, and patchwork made by the Hmong people. Hmong designs are characterized by geometric, symmetrical, intricate appliqué, reverse appliqué, and embroidery. Hmong pieces, called Pa Ndau, are not quilted.

Example of Hmong Appliqué

Hoop: an alternate kind of frame, much like a large embroidery hoop, for stretching a quilt during quilting. When tightening the hoop screw, allow some slack in the quilt and be certain all the layers are pulled evenly. Hoops are available in round or oval shapes in sizes from 8″ to 29″ (round) and up to 18″ x 27″ (oval).

Horizontal Row: a row of blocks, with or without sashing, that crosses the quilt at a 90° angle to the lengthwise edge. Many quilts made from blocks are constructed by joining blocks in horizontal rows and then joining the rows.

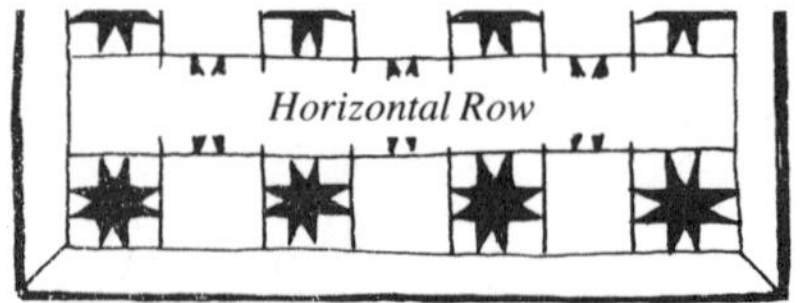

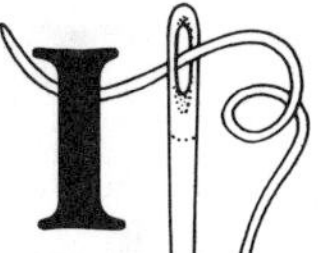

In-the-Ditch Quilting: a line of quilting stitches that is right next to a seam or around an appliqué patch on the side without seam allowances. In-the-ditch quilting is especially good for appliqué quilts because it makes the patches seem to puff up a bit.

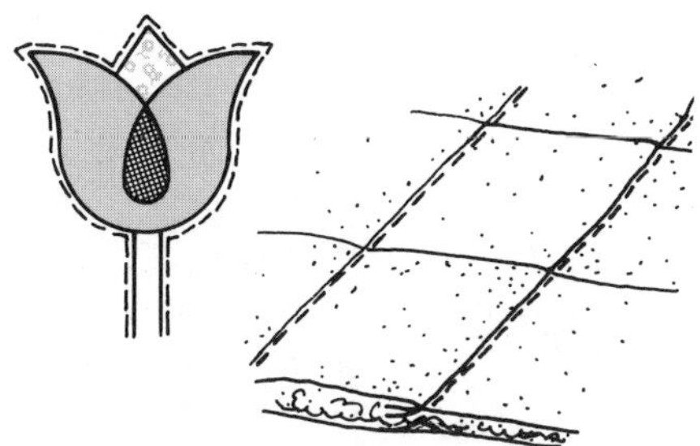

In-the-Ditch Quilting

Individual Binding Strips: four cut strips, one for each edge of the quilt, to be sewn on one at a time. Cut strips a few inches longer than the quilt's edges. Corners can be mitered or butted.

Individual Binding Strips Cut With Extra Length for Insurance

Insurance: the extra length (usually about 2″) allowed when cutting border strips in case the blocks or quilt center end up larger than expected. The extra length often will not be needed and will be cut away after the borders are sewn on.

Invisible Thread: nylon thread, available in clear or smoke color, that is sometimes used for machine appliqué and machine quilting. Select fine thread (size .004 is recommended); heavier thread is too stiff for use on quilts.

Ironing: moving an iron across fabric (wet or dry) to smooth and flatten it. Ironing is different than pressing, which is a lifting-and-lowering motion. Yardage is ironed before being marked and cut into patches or cut for lining. Patches and blocks are not ironed, but rather are pressed because pressing is not likely to stretch or distort them.

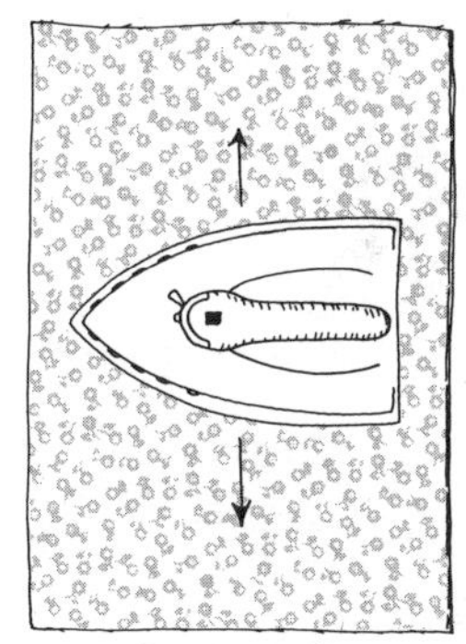

Ironing Fabric

Italian Cording: quilted channels that are stuffed with yarn or cording. See Trapunto.

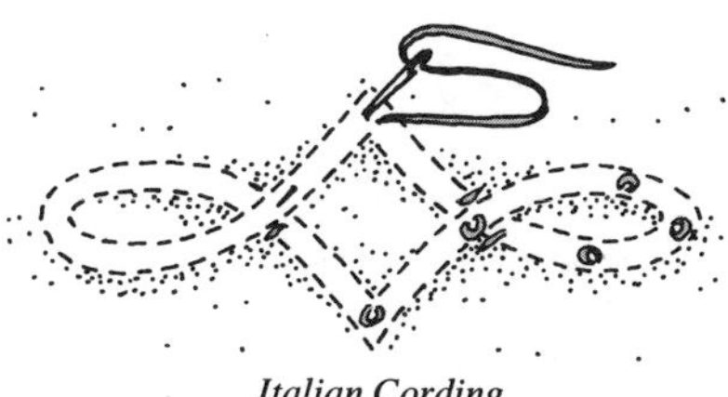

Italian Cording

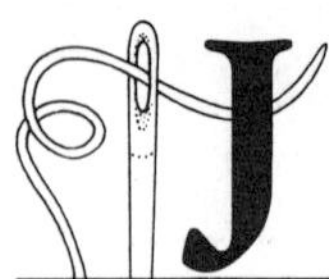

Join: to sew one patch, unit, or block to another.

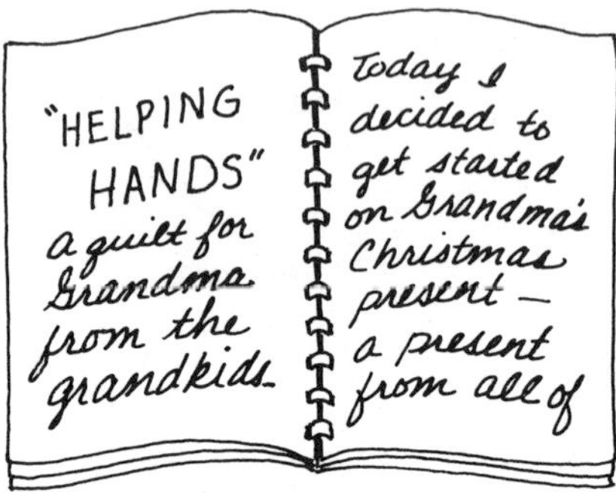

Writing a Journal
- *What happened in the news?*
- *Family activities?*
- *How did the quilt design evolve?*
- *How do you feel about making the quilt?*
- *What fabrics have you chosen?*

Journal: a remembrance book in which stories (and sometimes pictures) of quilts and quiltmakers are recorded. Some quiltmakers keep an individual journal for each quilt and give it away with the quilt; others keep one continuing journal.

Juried Shows: competitions or exhibitions that have a screening process to select the quilts to be on display. Jurying usually is done from slides, but it also can be done with the actual quilts. If the selection process will be done with slides, it is very important to provide the jurors with sharp, well-lit slides that show all of the quilt. Label slides as instructed in the show rules.

Juvenile Quilts: those with designs appropriate for children.

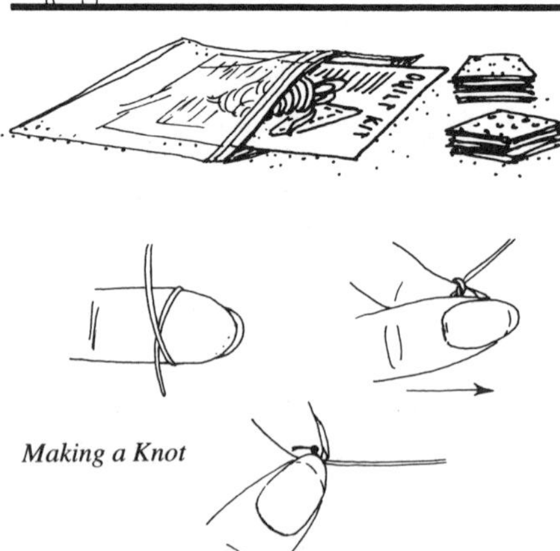

Making a Knot

King Bed: mattress size is 76″ x 80″.

Kit: a packaged assembly of fabric, pattern, and other items needed for making a quilt. Kits sometimes come with precut patches.

Knot: a tie in the end of thread for hand sewing; the knot begins the line of sewing and stops the thread from pulling out. Knots are optional; two or three backstitches also can be used to secure the beginning of thread.

Lap Quilting: see Quilt-As-You-Go Method.

Lattice Stripping: see Sashing.

Layering: assembling the quilt "sandwich." Working on a large, flat surface such as the floor or a table, spread out the lining (wrong side up), batting (smoothed over lining), and quilt top (placed over batting right side up). The layers are secured with basting stitches or with rustproof safety pins. (Straight pins can be used to temporarily secure the layers while the basting is done.) After quilting or tying, the basting or pins are removed.

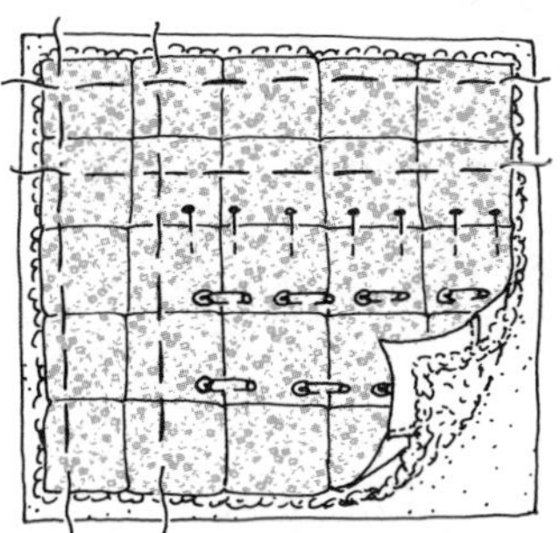

Layering a Quilt With Pins or Basting

Length of Borders: the cut dimension of border strips. To determine this dimension, measure the finished size of the quilt top (not including seam allowances or borders), and then add twice the finished width of the border (if corners will be mitered), seam allowances, and extra length for insurance if desired. If borders will have butted corners, the side border strips should measure the same length as the quilt top, including seam allowances.

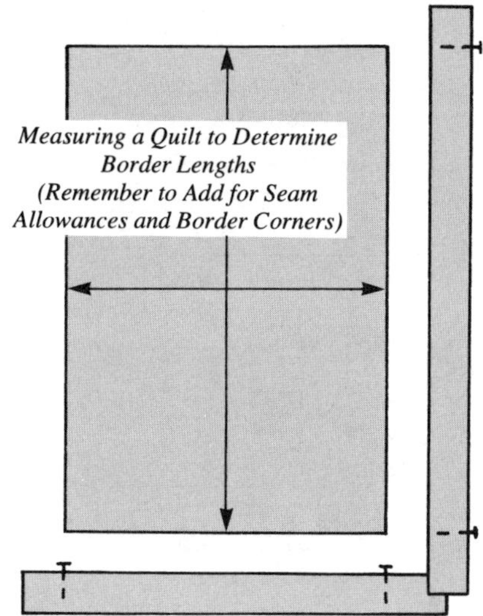

Measuring a Quilt to Determine Border Lengths (Remember to Add for Seam Allowances and Border Corners)

Lengthwise Grain: the fabric threads that are parallel to the selvedges, also called warp threads. Lengthwise grain has very little stretch, if any. Many quiltmakers prefer to cut borders and sashing on the lengthwise grain to avoid any stretch, even if the dimension needed is short enough to allow them to be cut on crosswise grain. Straight-grain binding usually is cut on lengthwise grain.

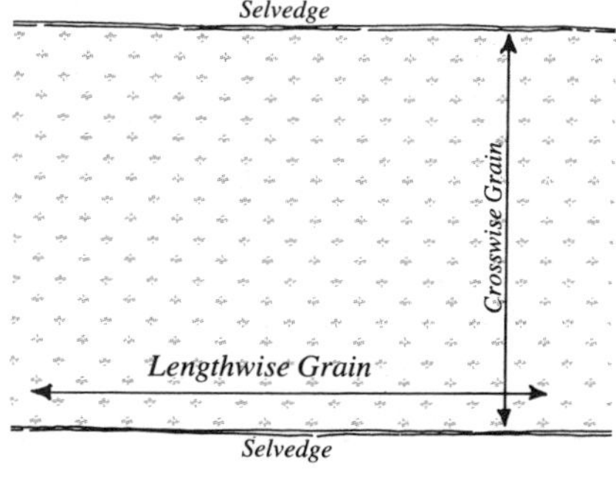

L

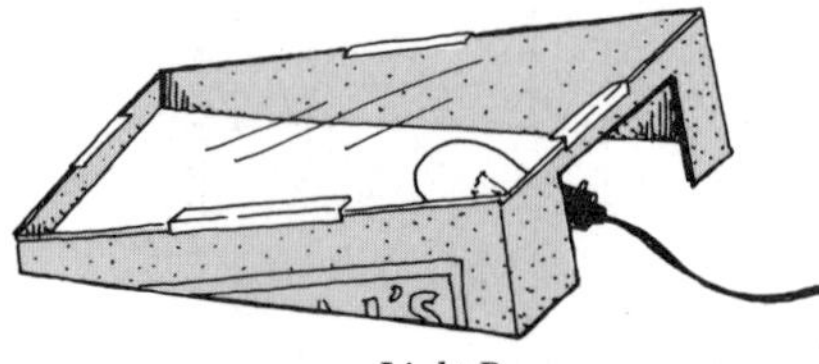

Light Box

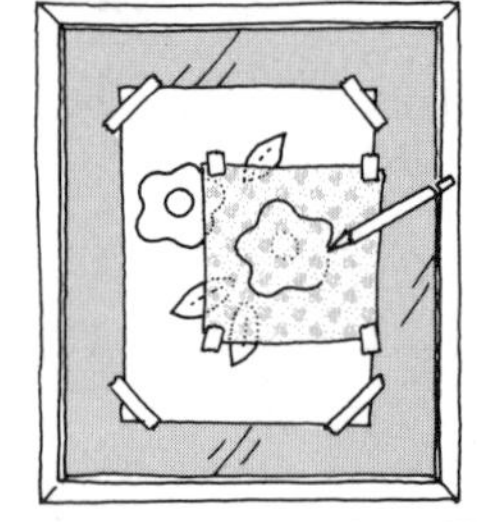

Pattern and Fabric Taped to a Window

Taped to a Television

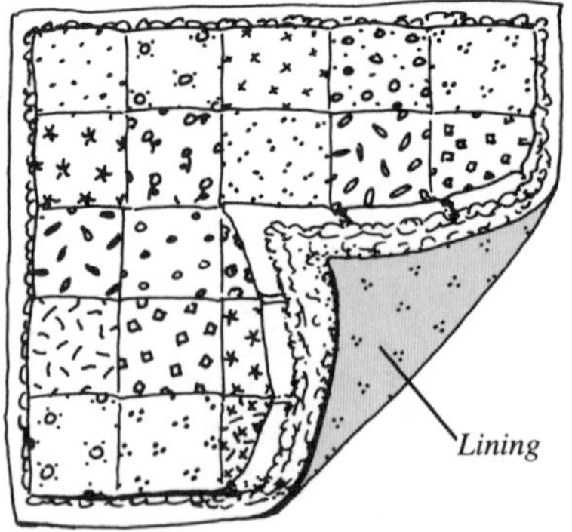

Light Box (or Table): a work surface that has translucent glass (or plastic) that is illuminated from underneath. A light box or its equivalent makes tracing designs onto fabric much easier. One way to substitute for using a light box is to tape the design pattern to a sunny window, tape the fabric over it, and then trace the design. Another handy trick for tracing a small pattern is to tape it to a television screen and tape the fabric over the design. Turn on the television to an unassigned channel (to get white "snow") and trace.

Light Fading: the loss of color density in fabric due to exposure to light. Sunlight is especially detrimental to the dyes in fabrics used to make quilts, but fluorescent lighting also is harmful. The ultraviolet rays that cause light fading can be filtered with special shields for windows and light fixtures, but most quiltmakers either avoid using a quilt in places exposed to excessive light or accept the inevitable fading that occurs with some colors and fabrics.

Lining: the bottom layer of the quilt. It usually is not pieced or appliquéd, although most bed-size quilts require that panels of fabric be joined to make the lining. Another word for lining is backing.

Lining Fabric: material chosen for the back of the quilt. If the quilt will be hand-quilted, select fabric that will be easy to quilt: soft, closely woven, 100 percent cotton. Quilts wider than about 40″ will require one or more seams in

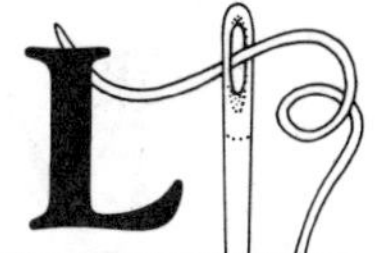

the lining unless extra-wide (90″) fabric is used. A print fabric will disguise the seam(s) and the quilting stitches, which could be less even on the back of the quilt than on the front.

Various Ways to Seam Lining

Lining Seams: those that join lengths of fabric to make a lining about 4″ larger than the quilt top. If two lengths of fabric are required for the lining, one seam can join two same-width panels or two seams can connect one wide panel and two narrower strips. It is preferable not to have the lining seam directly under a line of quilting because of the extra bulk of seam allowances. If the lining seam is stitched by machine (with a short stitch length), the seam allowances can be pressed open. The lining seam is usually positioned vertically but can run horizontally to conserve fabric (although some judges of quilt shows may take off points for this).

Linsey-Woolsey: an old term referring to fabric made of linen and wool. Also, the name is inaccurately applied to glazed-wool, whole-cloth quilts made during the 18th and early 19th centuries.

Loft: the thickness and springiness of quilt batting. High-loft batting is thick and bouncy; low-loft batting is thin and compact. Each batting manufacturer's product has a slightly different loft.

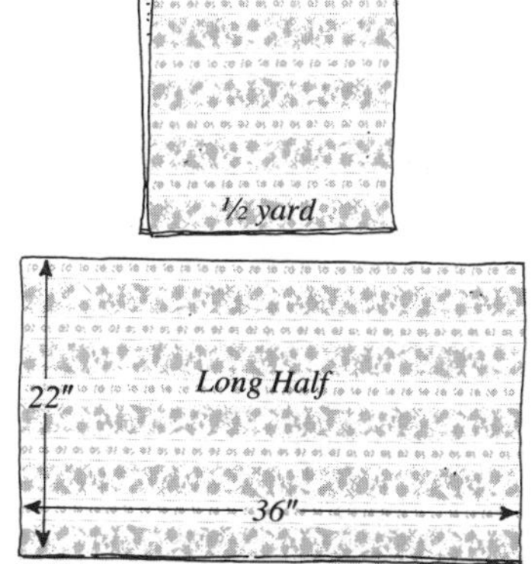

Long Half: a piece of fabric cut one yard long (36″) by half width (usually about 22″).

M

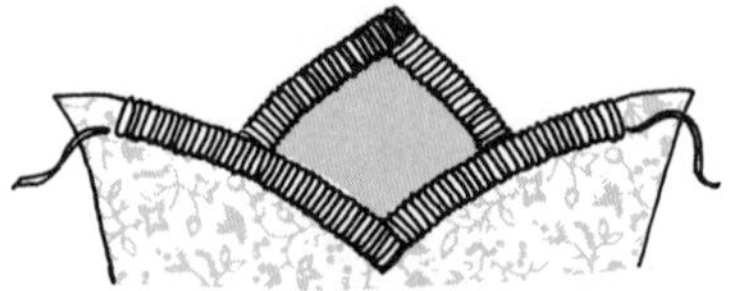

Machine Appliqué With Satin Stitch

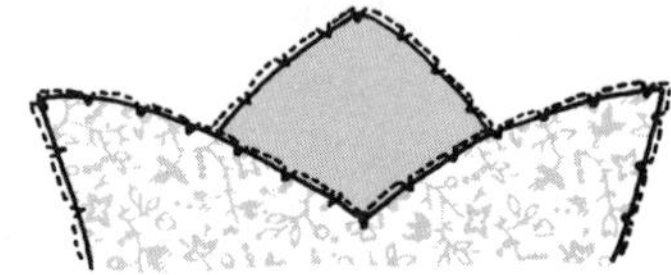

Machine Appliqué With Blind-Hem Stitch

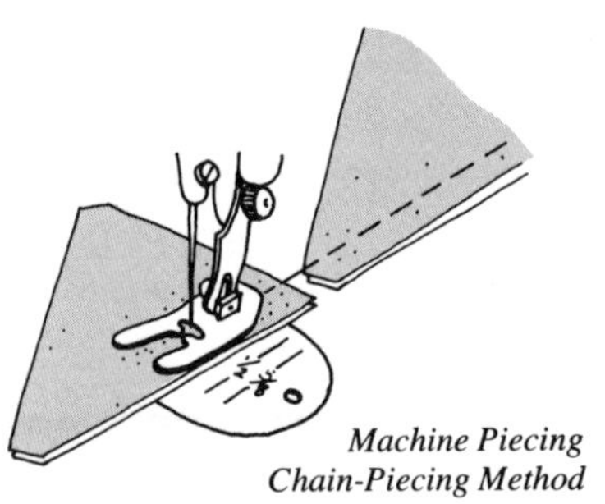

Machine Piecing
Chain-Piecing Method

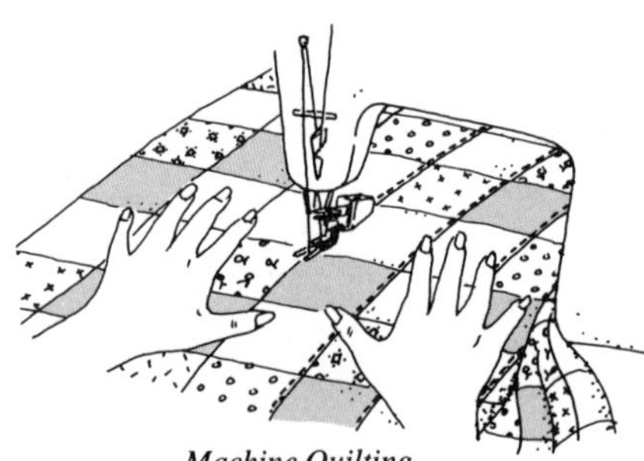

Machine Quilting

Darning Foot

Machine Appliqué: to apply patches with machine sewing. One technique uses satin stitch (close zigzag stitch) to define the patches with bold outlines. Patches for this method of machine appliqué usually do not include turn-under allowances. Another technique is similar to hand appliqué in its finished appearance; it uses invisible thread and blind-hem stitch. Prepare patches (turning under and basting the allowances) as you would for hand appliqué and pin or baste them in place. Set the machine on a very short stitch length and narrow width and work a blind-hem stitch around patches.

Machine Piecing: to sew patches together with a sewing machine. Machine piecing yields seams that are strong, and the work progresses quickly compared to hand piecing.

Machine Quilting: stitching with a sewing machine through all three layers of the quilt to fasten them and add decorative relief and texture to the quilt. Machine quilting is usually done with a walking foot that evenly feeds the quilt under the needle, or with a darning foot (with feed dogs lowered) that allows freedom to move the quilt in any direction.

Magnetic Pincushion: a magnetized surface for holding steel pins and needles. (Brass does not adhere to a magnet.) Manufacturers of computerized sewing machines recommend caution when using a magnetic pincushion because the magnetic field can make the machine perform erratically.

Marking Lines for Quilting: using a marker that leaves a removable line (soap sliver, water-erasable pen, or pencil) to lightly mark motifs for quilting. Marking can be done with slotted stencils, by tracing over a design (using a light source behind if necessary), or by marking around shapes. Marking is often done before the quilt layers are basted but it also can be done just before quilting. Many lines of quilting, such as those for outline quilting and around appliqué patches, need not be marked. Always be sure that the markings can be easily removed after the quilting is complete.

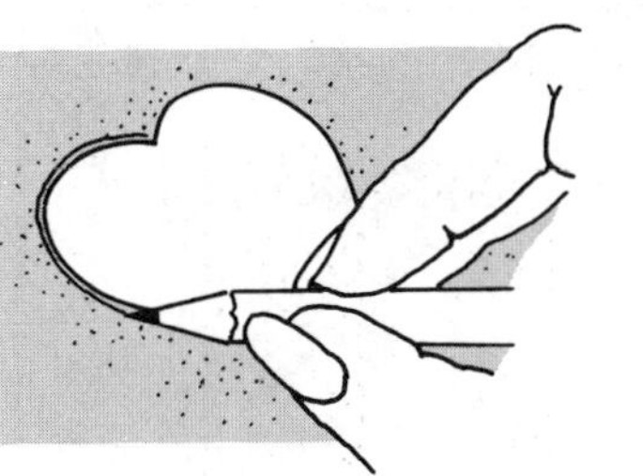

Marking Around a Stencil for Quilting

Marseilles Quilting: see Trapunto.

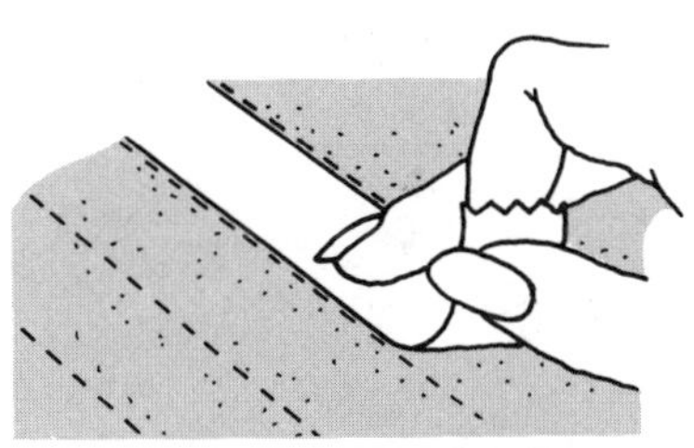

"Marking" With Masking Tape

Masking Tape: sticky tape available in hardware stores (in many widths) and in quilt shops (in ¼″ width) that is excellent for using to "mark" lines to be quilted, especially long straight lines and outline quilting ¼″ from seams. Just quilt next to the masking tape (on one or both sides), then peel it away. Sometimes tape can be used more than once; other times it won't be sticky enough to use again. It is better not to leave tape on a quilt for an extended period of time because it might leave a residue.

Meandering Quilting: see Stipple Quilting.

Measuring Across the Quilt Top: using a tape measure to record the length and width of the quilt top to determine the actual border lengths, which will possibly be different from

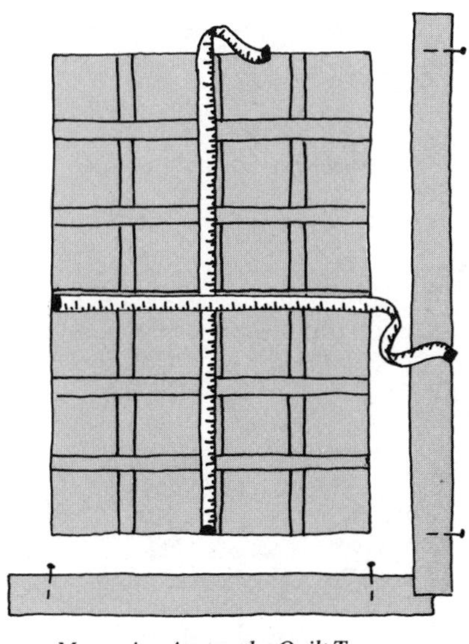

Measuring Across the Quilt Top Through the Center

An Example of a Medallion Quilt

what is expected because of inaccuracies in sewing. Measure through the center (not the edges) in both directions and record the measurements. Use pins to mark border strips to be these dimensions, allowing the excess length (needed for mitering) to be divided equally at the ends.

Medallion Quilts: those with a central block or design that is surrounded by multiple borders. Borders for medallion quilts are often pieced, but they can be plain, appliquéd, or a combination of techniques.

Memory Quilts: those which are made to remember people, places, events, or anything else.

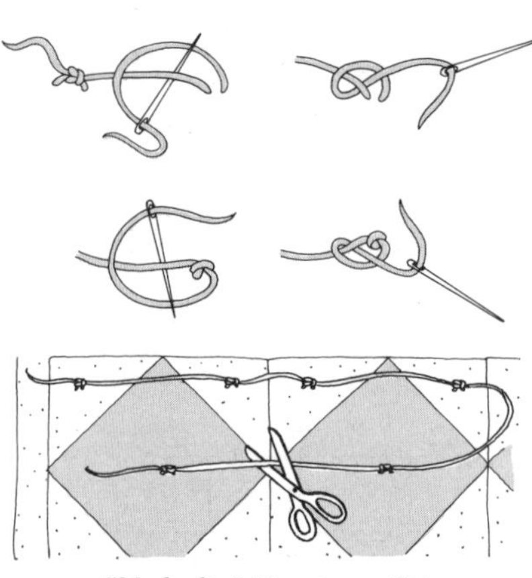

"Methodist" Knotting or Tying

Methodist Knotting (or Tying): a quick technique for tying a quilt. Thread needle with a long piece of floss, yarn, or narrow ribbon. Mark placement for ties with pins. At first pin, take a small stitch through all layers and tie a square knot. Proceed to the next pin and follow the steps shown above left to make the next knot. Clip thread to leave tails.

Miniature Quilts: those made in reduced size, often one-twelfth size to match the scale of dollhouses.

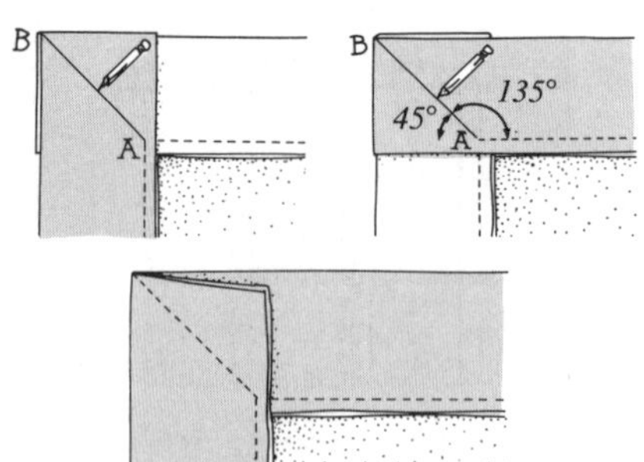

Marking and Sewing a Mitered Corner

Mitered Corner: a corner formed when two strips (block frame, border, or binding) are joined at a 45° angle. After sewing borders to edges of quilt top, mark a 135°/45° angle at the corner seam lines and stitch borders on the marked lines. Trim excess, leaving ¼″

seam allowances. Press both seam allowances toward one side (not open).

Mock-Up: a full-size (or nearly full-size) drawing of a block with fabric fastened in position. Many quiltmakers enjoy auditioning fabrics this way to find their favorite combinations.

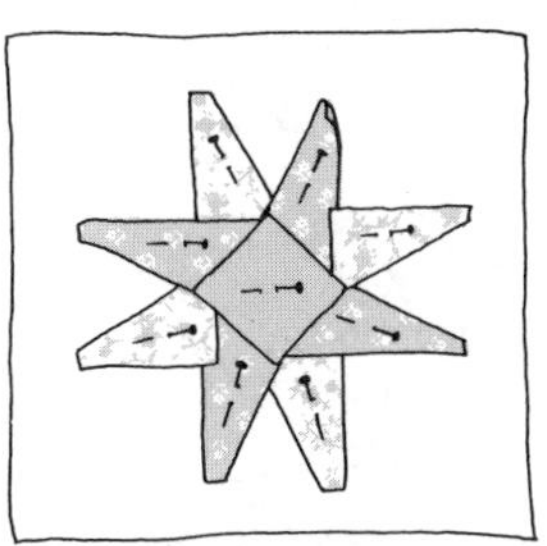

Mock-Up of Block

Molas: reverse-appliqué panels (and the blouses made from the panels) made by the Cuna people of the San Blas Islands. Molas have many layers of brightly colored fabric that form bold, graphic designs rich in feeling and symbolism.

An Example of a Mola

Motif: a design element that may (or may not) be repeated. For example, a cable is a motif that can be repeated in a quilted border; a feather wreath design might be used singly in the center of a medallion quilt.

Mourning Quilt: that which is made in memory of someone who has died. Some mourning quilts incorporate pieces of the clothing of the person being remembered. The making of a mourning quilt can be therapeutic in the grief process.

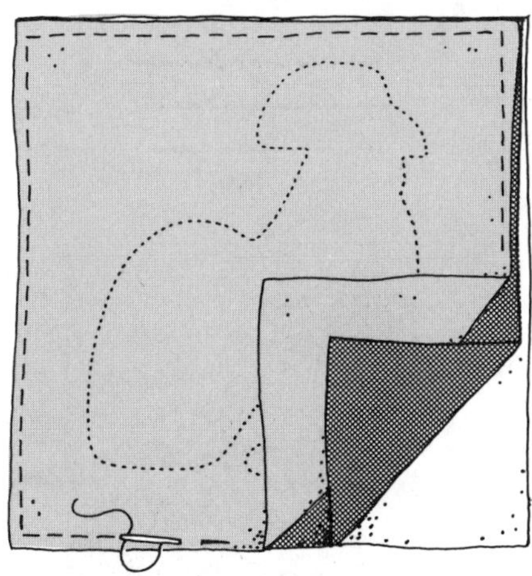

Basting the Layers in Preparation for Making a Mola

Muslin: cotton fabric of medium weight with a slightly coarser weave than that of broadcloth. Unbleached muslin is naturally off-white and has small brown flecks. Bleached muslin is white; muslin also can be dyed. Good-quality muslin is a favorite among quiltmakers; poor-quality muslin will wrinkle, allow the batting to "beard," and will not hold up well.

N

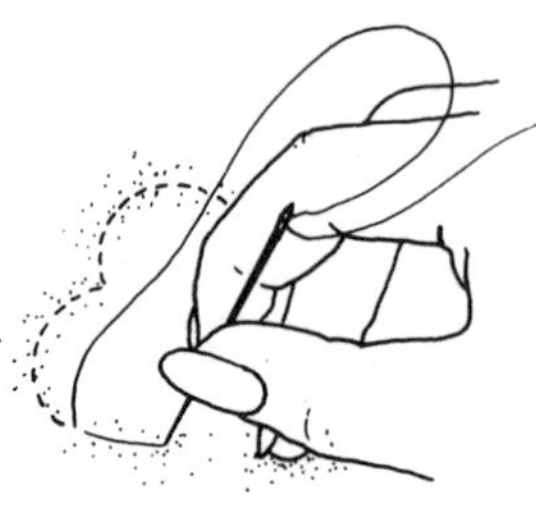

Needle Tracking

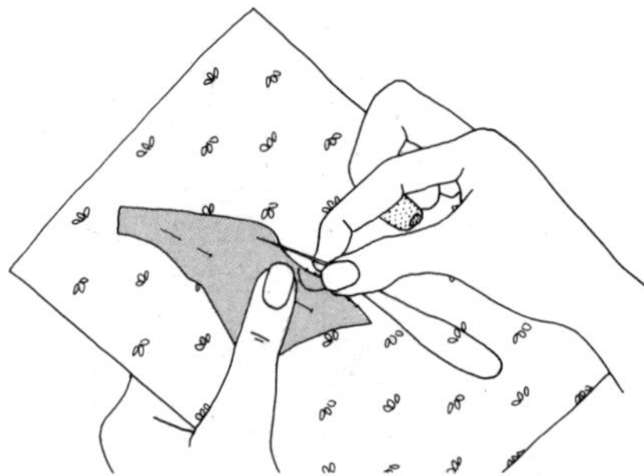

Needle Turning an Appliqué Patch

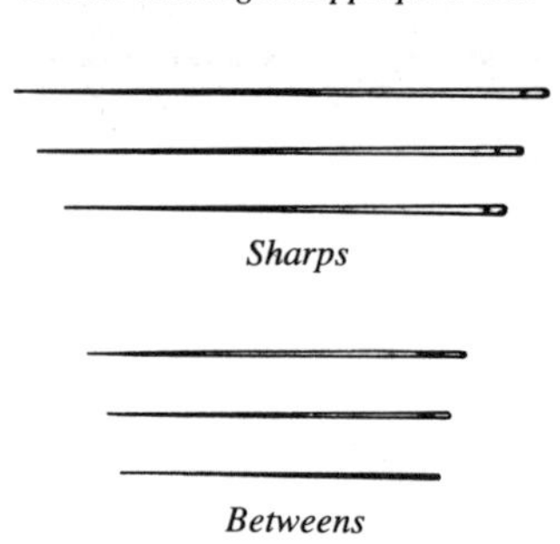

Sharps

Betweens

A Design Made With No-Baste Appliqué

Needle Tracking: marking a quilting design by scratching the quilt top with a pin or needle. Needle tracking is difficult to see on prints but it works well on solids. Because needle tracking disappears as the quilt is handled, it is best to mark the design just before quilting it.

Needle Turning: the use of the needle to gently turn under the allowance on hand-appliquéd patches. After turning under the allowance so that the marked line is barely out of sight, the thumb is used to "finger press" the crease before blindstitching.

Needlepunch Batting: that which is made commercially by pounding batting with needles to make a dense batting with low loft but firm body.

Needles: those used for piecing and appliqué are called sharps; those for hand quilting are called betweens. For hand or machine sewing, change needles frequently (as soon as you suspect the old needle is dull).

Needling: the action of working the needle through the layers when hand quilting. The term often is used to express the ease or difficulty of this action. Some fabrics and battings needle easily; others may be stiff or dense and needle with greater difficulty.

No-Baste Appliqué: a free-form technique in which no turn-under lines are marked on patches because the exact shape is not important. It progresses quickly because there is virtually no preparation needed before sewing.

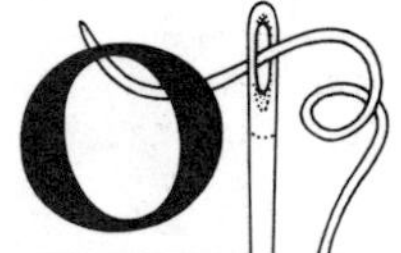

No-Mark Quilting: a term encompassing several techniques for which no marks are needed to guide the quilting. Echo quilting, in-the-ditch quilting, and outline quilting are three no-mark methods.

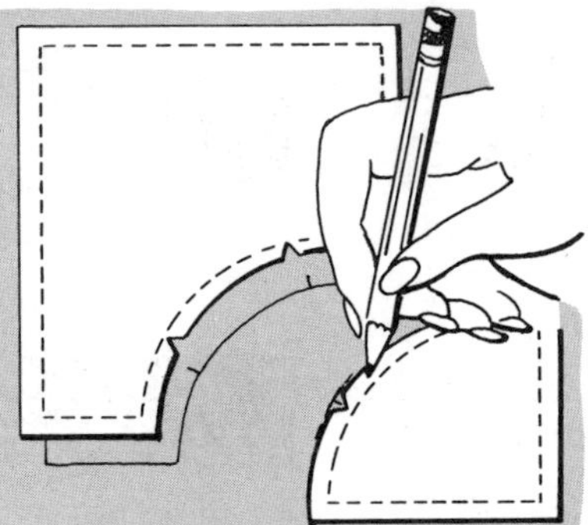
Marking Notches on Patches

Notches: lines marked across seam lines or in seam allowances to indicate points along the seam that should be matched. Notches are very helpful when sewing curved seams.

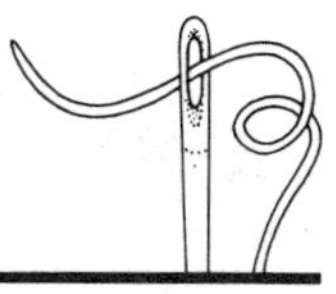

On Point: a term used to express the orientation of a quilt block (or any square) when its corners are placed up, down, and to the sides.

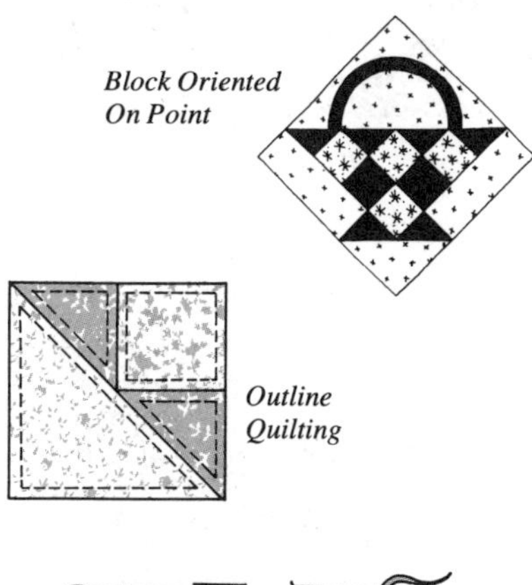
Block Oriented On Point

Outline Quilting

Outline Quilting: quilting that outlines patches in lines that are usually ¼″ from the patch seams, which places the quilting just beyond the area where the fabric layers in the seam allowance would add extra thickness. Many quilters use ¼″-wide masking tape as a guide in outline quilting.

Outline Stitch: a decorative embroidery stitch that forms a narrow line. Outline stitch is an excellent choice for flower stems and inscriptions.

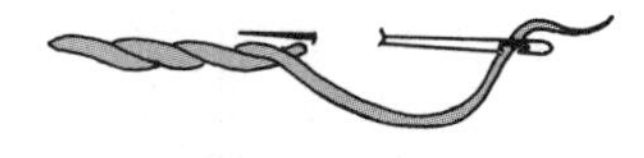
Outline Stitch

Overall Design: the effect created when blocks are combined in such a way (for example, with pieced sashing) to decrease the individuality of the blocks and produce a blended pattern such as the example illustrated at right.

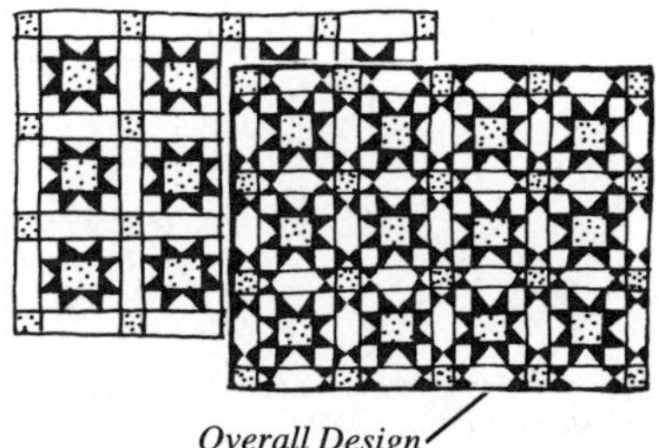
Overall Design

P

Partial Piecing

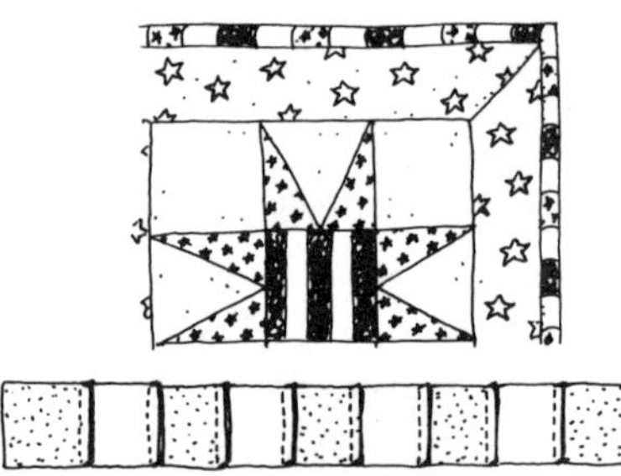

Patchwork Binding

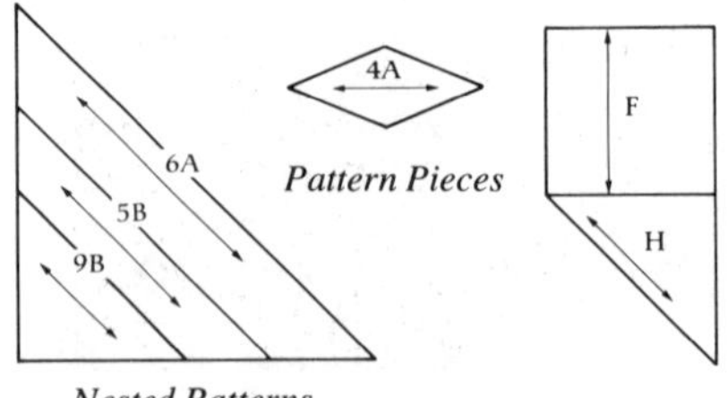

Pattern Pieces

Nested Patterns

Pa Ndau: see Hmong Needlework.

Palette: a quiltmaker's collection of fabric.

Paper Basting: see English Piecing.

Partial Piecing: a technique (suitable for only some block patterns) used to avoid setting in an angled patch. With this method the first two patches are sewn only part way. More patches are added and, after joining the last patch of a unit or the block, the partial seam is completed.

Patch: a fabric piece to be sewn into a quilt. Typically, patches are joined to make units, units are joined to make blocks, and blocks are sewn with other components such as sashes and borders to complete the quilt top.

Patchwork: a term that can apply to appliqué, but more often indicates pieced work.

Patchwork Binding: pieced binding made from square or rectangular patches sewn side by side to make long strips. Remember to allow for seam allowances when figuring the cut size of patches. Patchwork binding works best when applied as single binding because it is too bulky to be applied as double binding. See Single Binding.

Pattern: the printed shapes and directions for making a project. Pattern pieces are the actual paper shapes used to make templates for marking and cutting patches.

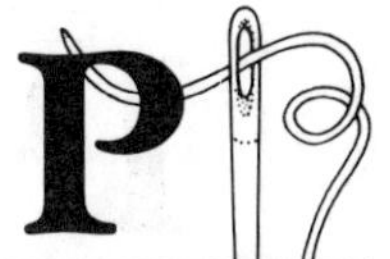

Pearl Cotton: a shiny cotton thread used for embroidery and tying comforters. Pearl cotton comes in many colors and three sizes: 3 (thick), 5 (medium), and 8 (thin).

An Example of a Picture Quilt

Pencil: a tool used at several stages of quiltmaking. Lead or colored pencils are often used to mark patches for cutting and piecing, and they may be used to mark designs for quilting. A hard lead is a good choice for marking quilting because it will not smudge. A mechanical pencil is very helpful because it never needs sharpening and it marks a consistently narrow line. Always make markings that are no darker than necessary.

Photo Transfer: any of several techniques in which a photo image is printed on fabric for use in a quilt. Photo transfers are especially suited to family history quilts and memory quilts. Also see Cyanotype Printing.

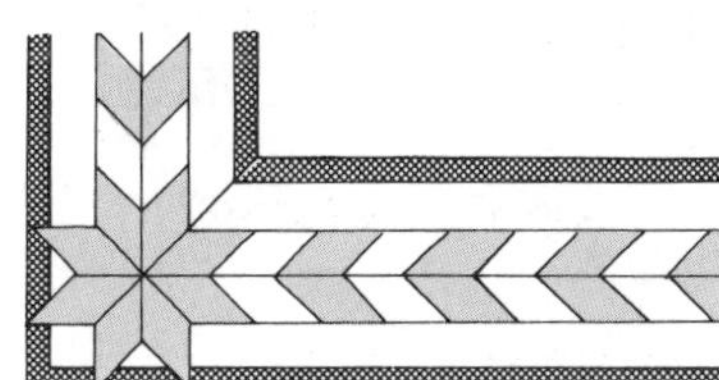

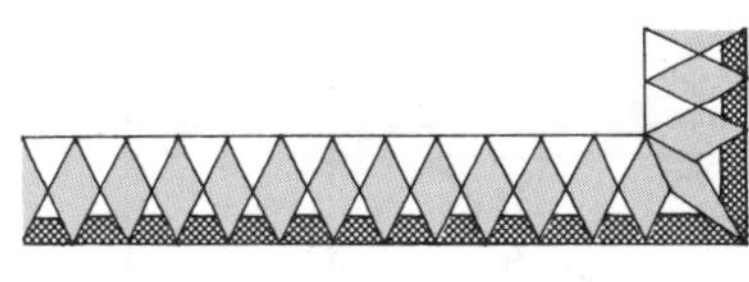

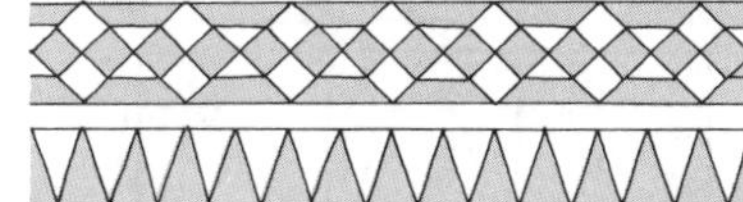
Pieced Borders

Picture Quilt: a quilt that depicts something from nature or a story, whether real or imaginary. Picture quilts can be pieced, although more of them are appliquéd because of the flexibility of that technique.

Pieced Borders: those made from patches, which are assembled with the same methods as for pieced blocks. Graph paper will be very helpful in planning pieced borders.

Pieced Frames: those made from patches. Pieced frames can be simple with squares sewn at each corner, or

Pieced Frame

P

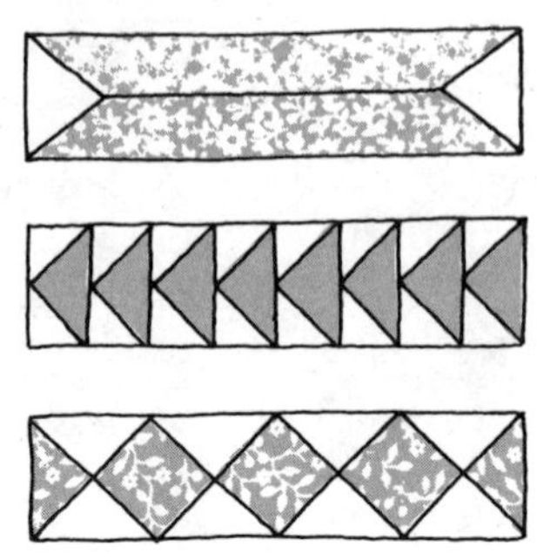
Pieced Sashing

they can be more complex with many patches.

Pieced Sashing: sashing that is divided into smaller patches to create additional design interest. Pieced sashing can offer endless possibilities for changing the look of traditional quilt blocks or new designs, whether they are pieced or appliquéd. Patches for pieced sashing are marked, cut, and sewn just as those for quilt blocks.

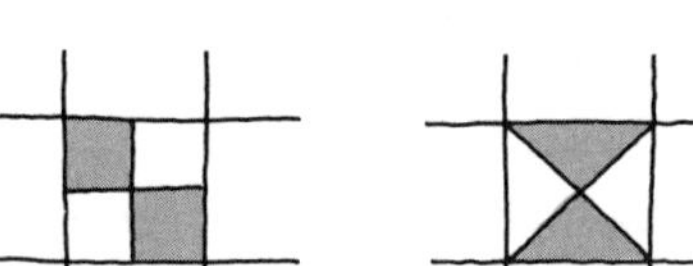
Pieced Setting Square

Pieced Setting Squares: miniature quilt blocks sewn between sashes at block intersections. Pieced setting squares usually have a simple design because of their small size.

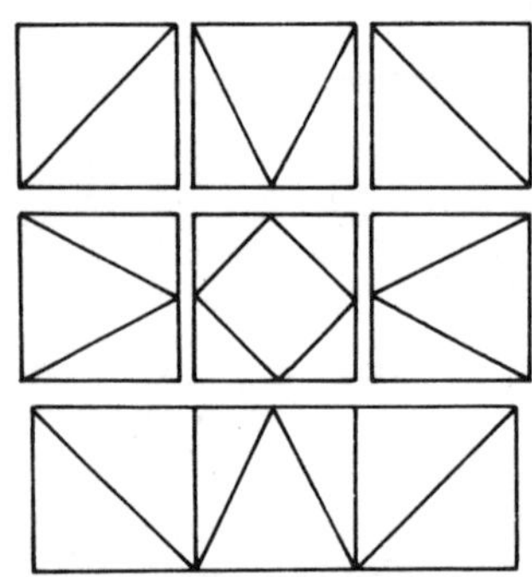
"Exploded" Piecing Diagram

Piecing: joining with seams the patches, units, blocks, or other elements of a quilt top. Piecing can be done with hand sewing or with machine stitching. Patches to be pieced usually have straight edges, but they also can be curved.

Piecing Diagram: a drawing of the block that indicates the best order for piecing. Piecing diagrams are "exploded," with spaces between unit parts of the block.

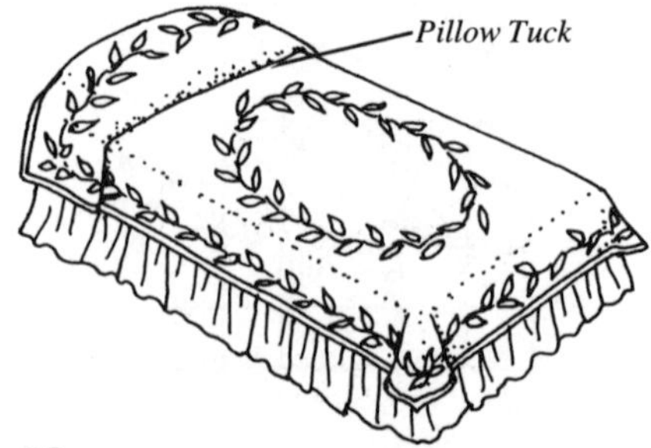

Pillow Tuck: the part of the quilt that forms a fold underneath the bed pillows. Sometimes quiltmakers add extra length to allow for the pillow tuck; occasionally the design is planned to have one large motif for the top of the bed and a smaller design for the pillows with a plain area where the pillow tuck will be.

Pin Basting: using straight pins (long "quilting" pins) or rustproof safety pins to secure the three layers of the quilt instead of basting with running stitches. Pin basting is an especially good choice for quilts to be tied or machine quilted because the pins need not stay in the quilt for a long time.

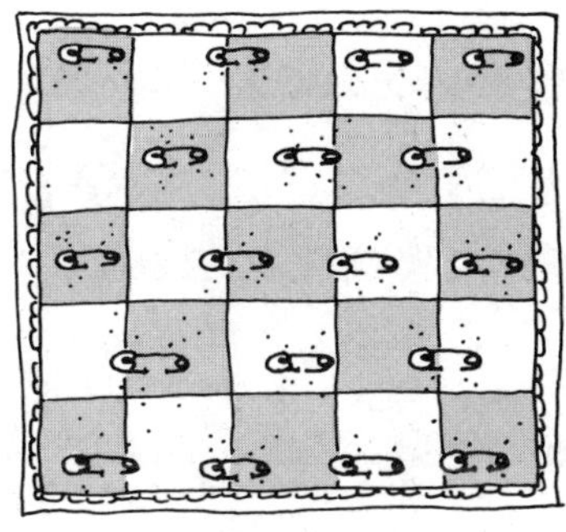

Pin Basting

Pin Marking: a method of indicating with pins on long sashes where the short sashes and blocks should match. Careful measuring and marking with pins will assure that the blocks and sashes line up visually, and it also will help control blocks that may vary in size by making them all conform to the sashing.

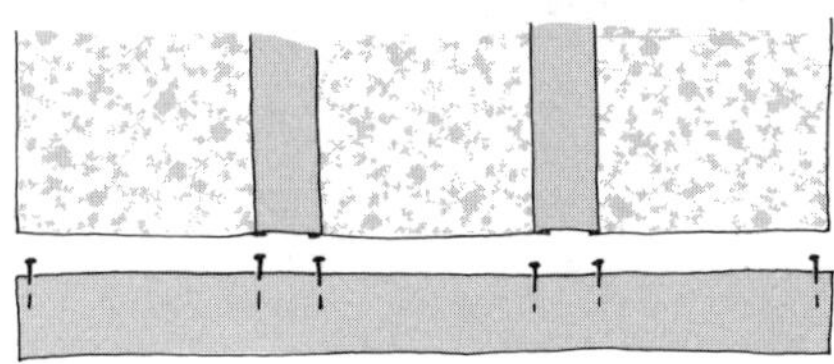
Pin Marking

Ping Pong Table: an ideal surface for basting a quilt. (Remove the net.)

Pinning Binding to Quilt: a step done with the quilt lying flat on a table or the floor. Allow the quilt to lie naturally, without stretching the edges. Pin the binding in place, right side down on the front of the quilt, with pins perpendicular to the quilt's edge. If making continuous binding, you may want to pin only one edge, sew to the corner, then lay out quilt again and pin the next edge.

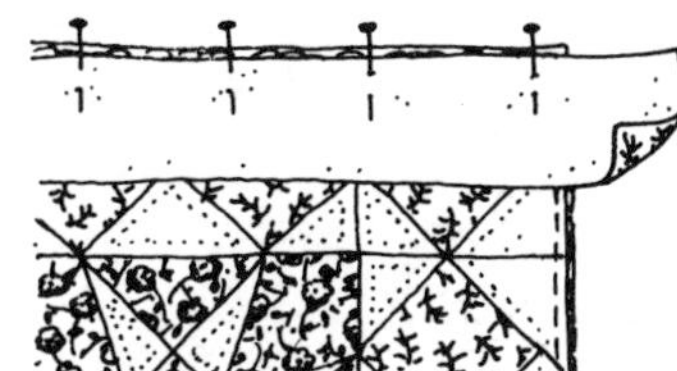
Pinning Binding to a Quilt

Placement Guidelines: pressed or basted lines on the background fabric to help in placing patches. Guidelines are especially useful for symmetrical blocks where precise placement of patches is needed for good results.

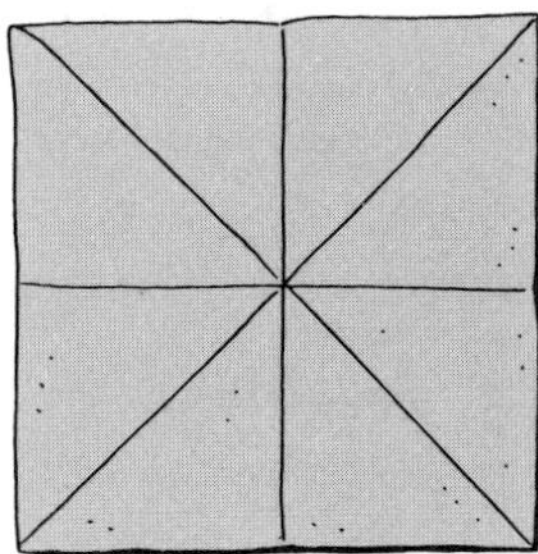
Placement Guidelines

Plain (Unpieced) Borders: those

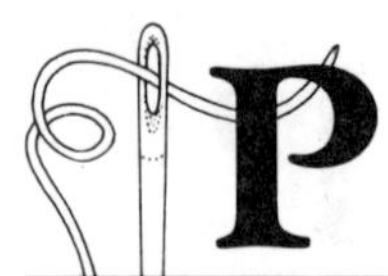

made from strips of fabric joined at the corners, whether butted or mitered.

Plain Borders on a Juvenile Quilt

Ply: the individual thread used to make yarn, sewing thread, or a strand of embroidery floss. Floss comes in six strands; each strand is two-ply. Sewing thread is usually two-ply. Bulky yarn for trapunto is three-ply; one or two plies may be used at one time.

Polished Cotton: cotton fabric with a shiny finish similar to chintz. The shine will probably wear off or wash out eventually.

Polyester Batting: the top-selling filler for quilts today, made from generic polyester fiber or trade names such as Dacron. Polyester batting, when bonded or glazed (as most are), is lightweight, easy to quilt, and does not readily shift or bunch as cotton batting will. It is available in several weights from "light" to "fat" and various sizes from crib to king. Many quilt shops also sell polyester batting by the yard.

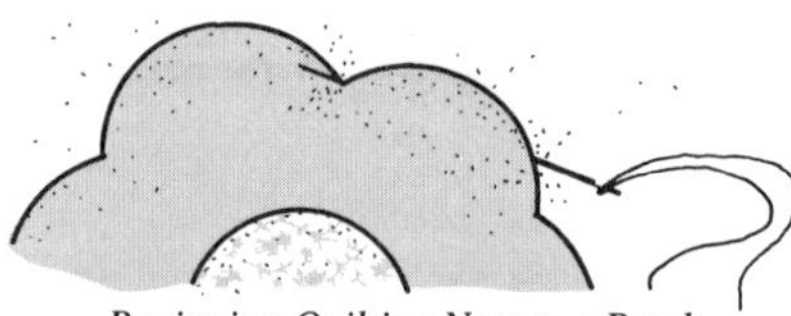
Beginning Quilting Next to a Patch

Polyester Fleece: flat, compact batting that is needlepunched. It is sold by the yard and can be used for a variety of craft projects and quilted wall hangings.

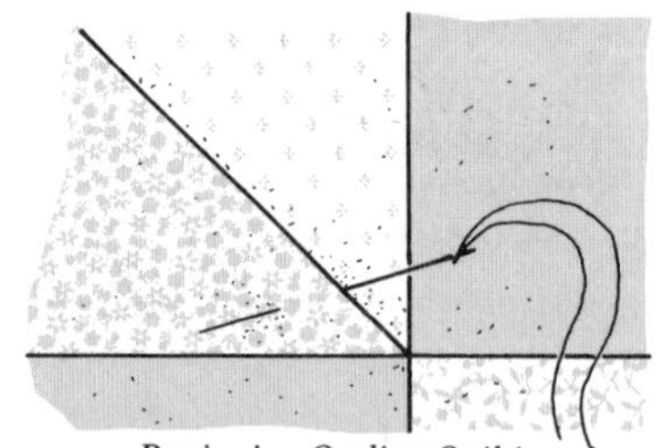
Beginning Outline Quilting

Popping the Knot: a technique for burying the knotted end of the quilting thread inside the quilt. The needle (with knotted thread) can either be slid between the stitches of a seam with the needle brought through the quilt top at the beginning point, or the knot can be popped into the quilt batting by giving

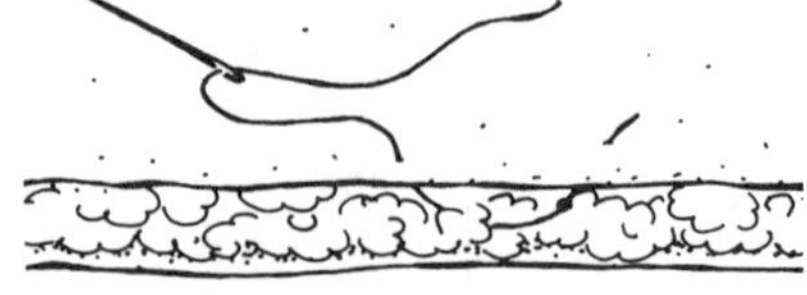
Popping the Knot to Begin a Line of Quilting

the first stitch a gentle tug. When reaching the end of the thread, make a knot on the surface of the quilt top and insert the needle back through the exact hole through which it last came. Give a little tug and the knot will pop into the batting.

Portuguese Hem: see Prairie Points.

Postage Stamp Quilts: those made from scraps cut in small squares or rectangles the size of postage stamps. These quilts often are picture quilts and can be made following charted designs such as those sold for counted cross stitch.

Poverty Piecing: the use of very small scraps of fabric by piecing them together before cutting out a patch, with the result that patches have seams in them.

Prairie Points: folded squares of fabric that form triangles, which are placed side by side or sewn together to make a zigzag edging on quilts. Quilts with a prairie-point edge do not need binding because they are sewn between the turned-under edges of the quilt top and quilt lining. Prairie points are also called Portuguese hem.

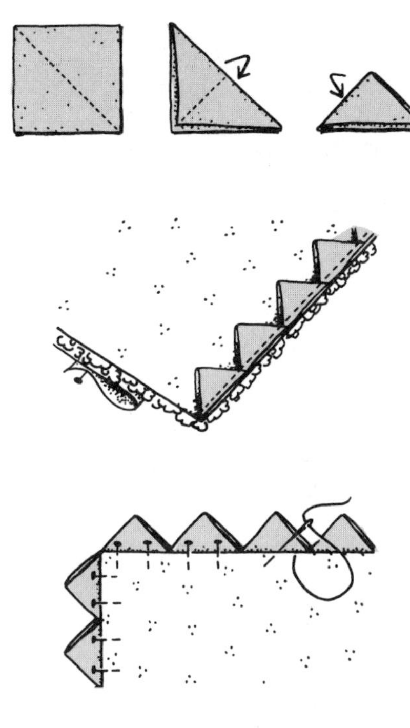

Prairie Point Edging

Preparing Quilt Edges for Binding: trimming lining and batting to extend about ⅛″ beyond the quilt top. Baste inside the perimeter seam allowance to hold the layers flat.

Press: lifting and placing the iron to flatten seam allowances and fabric.

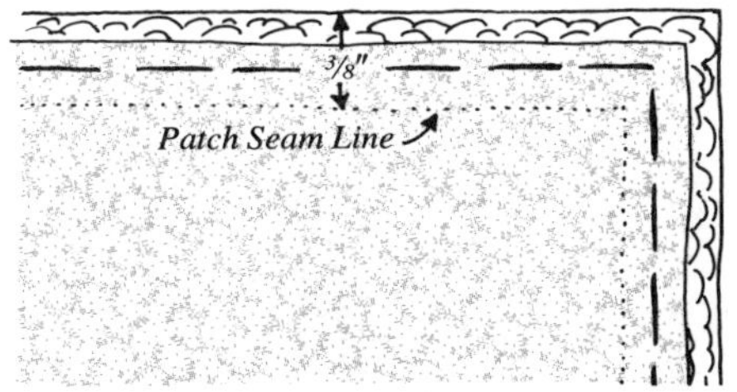

The Edge of a Quilt Prepared for Binding

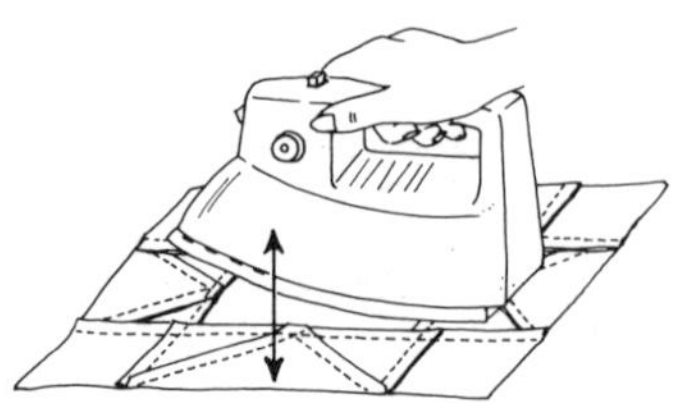

Lifting and Placing Iron When Pressing

Pressing can be done with or without steam. Do not move the iron back and forth on a patch or quilt block as this may stretch and distort the fabric.

Pressed Piecing: a block-construction technique that is worked on a foundation fabric. One patch is placed face up on the foundation, the next patch to be added is placed face down on the first patch, and the patches are stitched through all three layers. The second patch is folded out to be face up, then the next patch is positioned face down, and it is sewn. A variation of pressed piecing uses pattern lines marked on the underneath side of the foundation fabric, and the stitching is done from this back side. Pressed piecing is one method used for making Log Cabin, Pineapple, and Crazy quilt blocks.

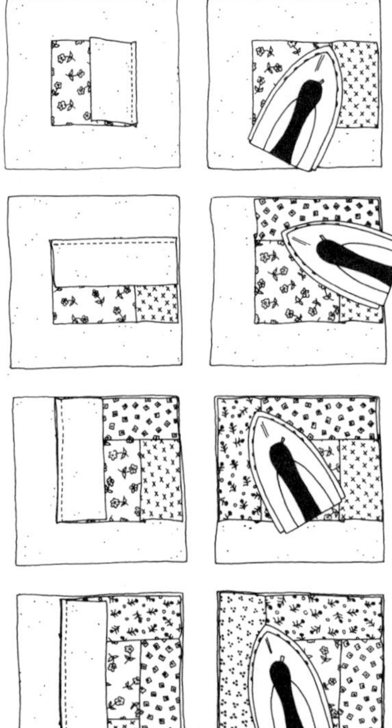

Pressed Piecing

Presser Foot: the part of a sewing machine that touches the fabric and holds it flat against the throat plate.

Pressing Surface: usually an ironing board, but this also can be a thick towel placed over a heat-proof surface.

Prewashing Fabric: the rinsing of fabric in hot water (with or without a little detergent) to shrink it and check for color bleeding. Fabrics should be rinsed one piece at a time to check for colorfastness. If the dye runs, continue rinsing until it stops bleeding. Fabric can be dried by machine or may be hung on a clothesline to dry. Large pieces of fabric can be washed and dried by machine after checking colorfastness. Iron fabric (using steam) to smooth it.

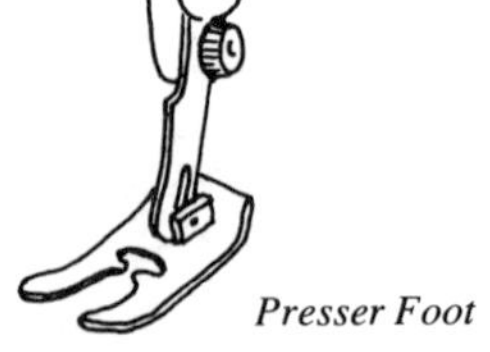

Presser Foot

Progressive Quilts: those made as group projects where one person begins a quilt and passes it along to the next person, who adds something (often appliqué or embroidery) and passes it along to the next person. The work continues until everyone involved has had a turn and the quilt is finished. Some quilt groups establish rules or guidelines before beginning a progressive quilt.

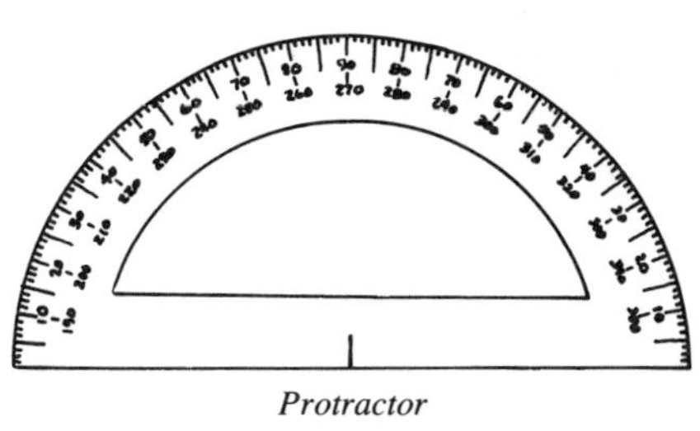
Protractor

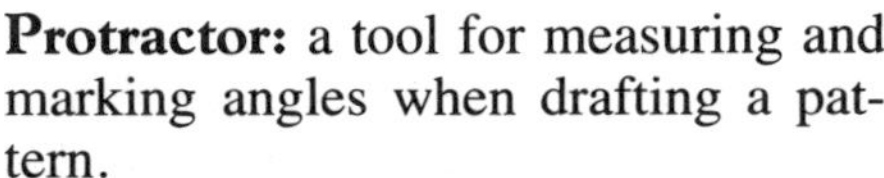
Protractor: a tool for measuring and marking angles when drafting a pattern.

Puff Patches: small pillows that are made, stuffed, and joined to make a thick comforter. See Biscuit (Puff) Quilting.

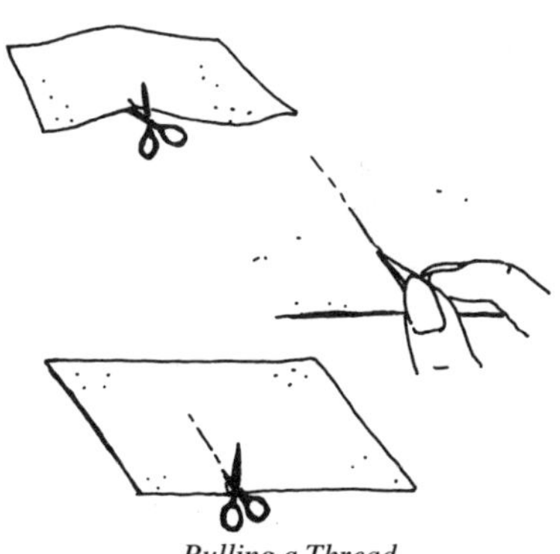
Pulling a Thread

Pulling a Thread: a sure (albeit slow) method for finding the exact straight of grain. Snip the end of the fabric for about an inch, then ravel one thread and pull on it gently. The thread will "run," giving a line on which to cut. The "run" will probably be only a few inches long, then another thread can be pulled to continue the line.

Putting In: mounting a quilt in a frame for hand quilting. Sometimes the three layers (lining, batting, and quilt top) are basted before putting in; other times the lining is fastened to the frame, the batting is spread out on top of the lining, and the quilt top is added before basting the layers in the frame. The task of mounting a quilt in a frame is made easier if two or three people are available to help.

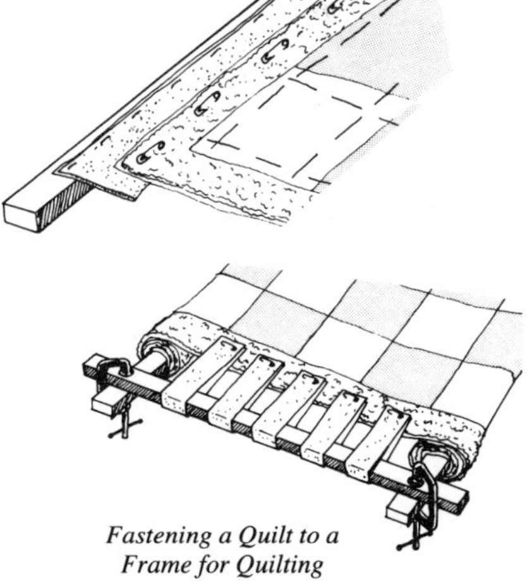
Fastening a Quilt to a Frame for Quilting

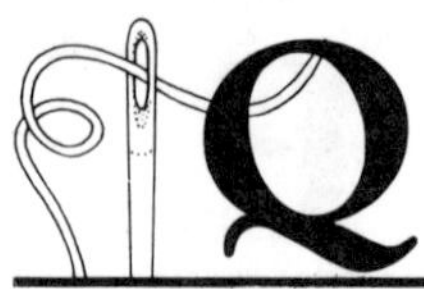

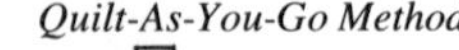

Quilt-As-You-Go Method

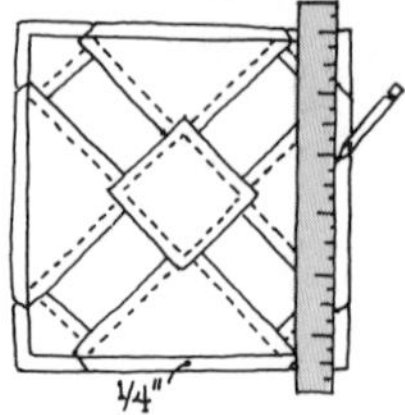

Mark seam line all around block.

Cut lining same size as block. Cut batting 1/4" smaller all around.

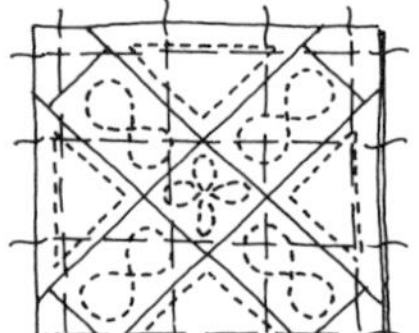

Baste three layers together and quilt.

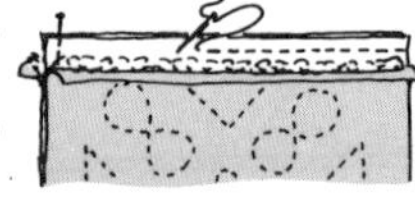

With right sides together, join blocks, sewing through top layers only.

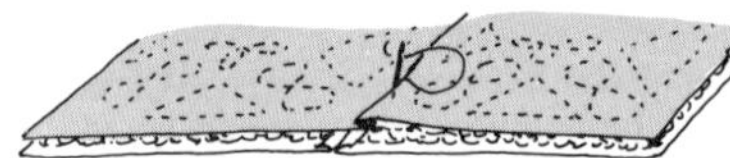

Fold under lining and blindstitch closed. Continue adding blocks in this manner.

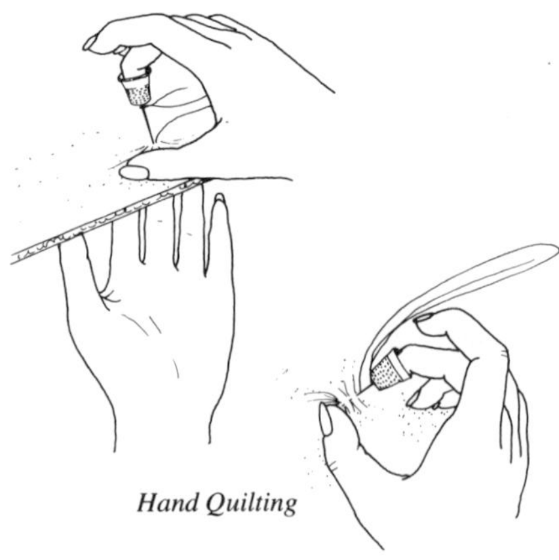

Hand Quilting

Queen Bed: mattress size is 60″ x 80″.

Quilt: a layered and stitched construction, usually comprised of lining, filler, and top. The term has come to mean different things now than in centuries past, incorporating a wide variety of styles, techniques, and end results.

Quilt-As-You-Go Method: a process of quiltmaking where each block is pieced or appliquéd and quilted before being sewn to other blocks. Each block can be completed one at a time, making the process easily portable.

Quilt Top: the upper layer of the quilt that is usually pieced, appliquéd, embroidered, or any combination of techniques. It is often made from blocks and may incorporate sashes, setting squares, and borders. Quilting usually is planned to accent the design of the quilt top although the quilting itself can be the primary design feature.

Quilting: the stitching that holds the quilt's three layers together. Quilting adds texture and design motifs to the quilt. Quilting can be done by hand with a running stitch or by machine sewing. Long, straight lines of quilting are particularly susceptible to breaking. For this reason, it is a good idea to change directions every few inches so that one-directional stress will not weaken the lines of quilting.

Quilting Bee: a social, group effort to work on one or more quilts, usually at the hand-quilting step. Good conver-

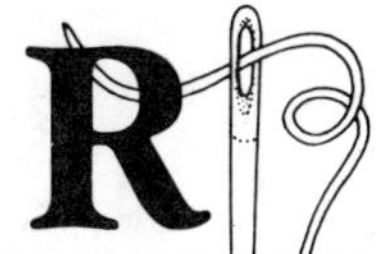

sation and shared food frequently are important elements of a quilting bee.

Quilting Thread

Quilting Thread: special thread that is extra strong for hand quilting. Regular sewing thread can be used for quilting (especially in short lengths) and can be coated with beeswax for strength, although it will not hold up under constant use as well as quilting thread. The thread color can be any that enhances the quilt top and may, in fact, change within the quilt. Some quiltmakers select a color that will blend in; others choose one that will contrast with the fabric(s) and show off the quilting.

Sewing Thread and Beeswax

Quiltist: a term occasionally used to describe a quilt artist.

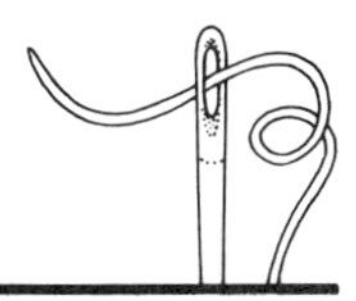

Raw Edges: those that are not turned under or sewn and which will fray if left unfinished.

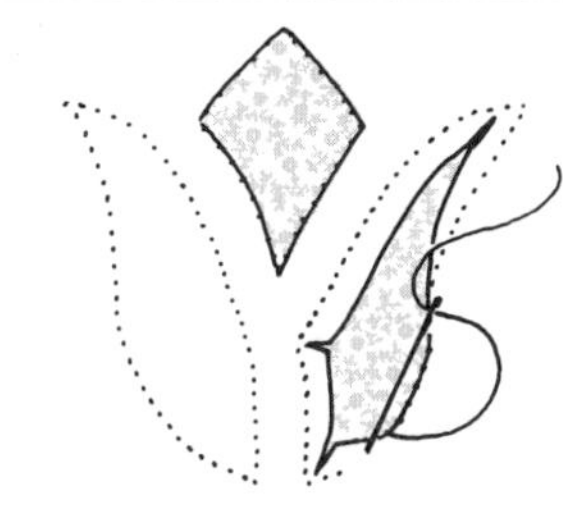
Reverse Appliqué

Reverse Appliqué: the cutting, turning under, and blindstitching of a top layer of fabric to reveal a shape created by the exposed underlayer of fabric. Reverse appliqué is especially useful when shapes are very small and when an illusion of depth is desired.

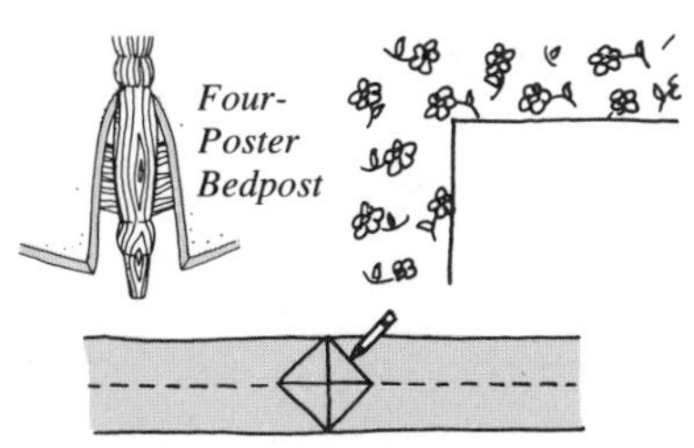

Reverse-Miter Binding

Reverse-Miter Binding: that which is used on an inside corner, such as on a quilt made for a four-poster bed to accommodate the bedposts. After cutting the binding strip, mark a square (on point) on the wrong side of the strip at

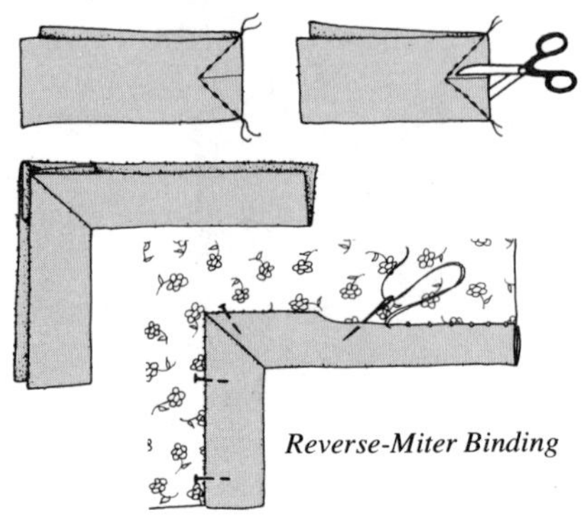
Reverse-Miter Binding

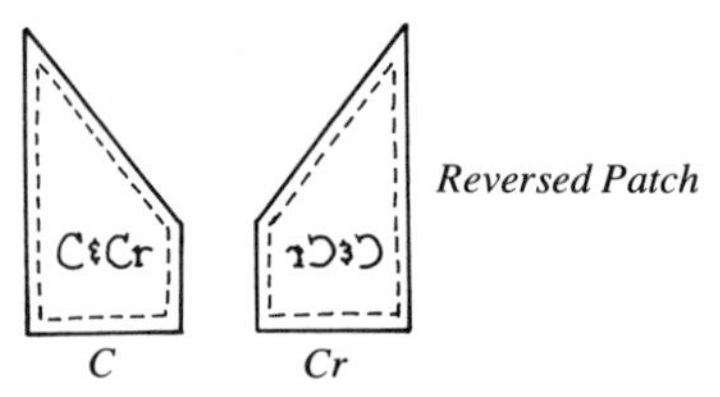

Reversed Patch

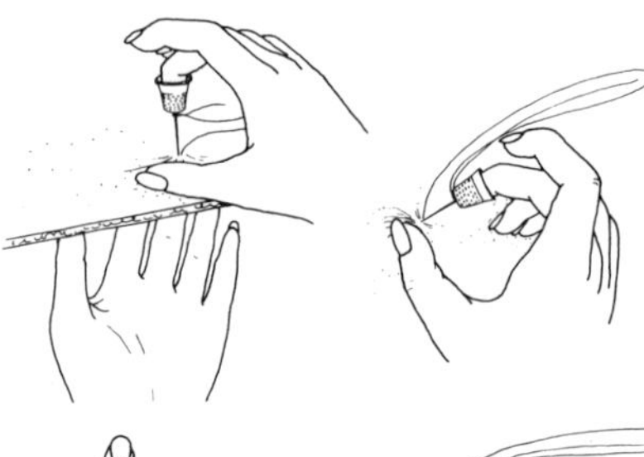

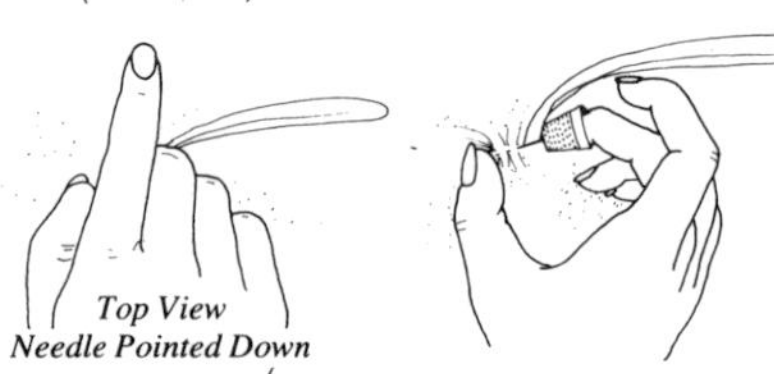

Rocking Motion for Hand Quilting

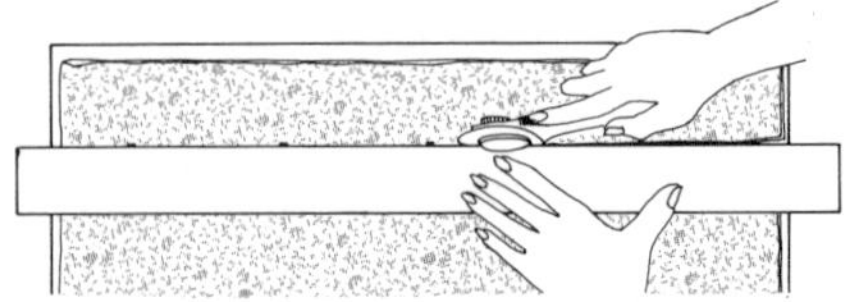
Rotary Cutting With a Mat Underneath Fabric

the place where the miter is needed, fold the binding strip crosswise with right sides together as shown, and stitch on the marked lines. Clip the dart indentation. Turn the binding right side out and fold it lengthwise; the binding strip will form a 90° angle. Pin the binding in place, turn under the allowance, and hand stitch the front and the back.

Reversed Patch: a patch that is a mirror image of another patch. Often such patches are indicated by an "r" following the patch letter. Turn the template over (reverse it) when marking a reversed patch.

Right Side of Fabric: the side that has the print or finish and will show in the finished quilt. Solid fabrics usually do not have right and wrong sides since both sides look the same.

Rippled Binding: a problem caused by stretching the binding (especially if it is bias) or the edge of the quilt.

Rocking Motion: a technique for hand quilting where the needle is pushed with the middle finger of the sewing hand and is guided with the hand underneath the quilt. The needle should be aligned with the finger almost as if it were an extension of the finger. When the alignment is not straight, the needle will slip off the thimble. The sewing hand rocks 90°, from pointing the needle straight down into the quilt to positioning the needle horizontally.

Rotary Cutting: a method recommended for cutting long strips because

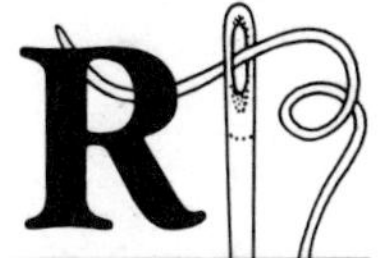

the rotary cutter allows fast, accurate cutting through several layers of fabric. Always use a cutting mat underneath a rotary cutter.

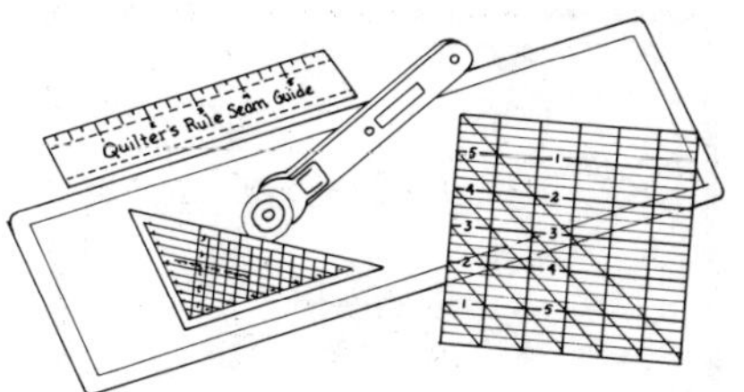

Rotary Cutter With Mat and Templates

Rounded Corners and Edges: a quilt's curved perimeter, which requires bias binding that can stretch and lie flat.

Rows: horizontal or vertical units of a quilt. Blocks are usually sewn to make rows, then rows are joined to construct the quilt top.

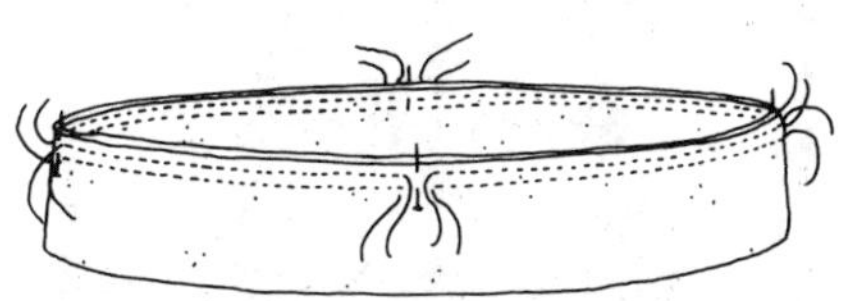

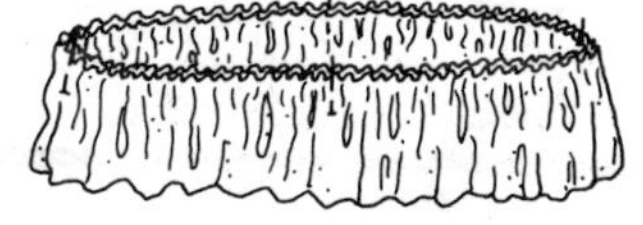

Ruffled Edging: a novelty edge finish for quilts in which a long strip of fabric (which is often pieced) is folded wrong sides together, gathered along the raw edges, and sewn between the turned-under edges of the quilt top and the quilt lining. Before gathering, the strip of fabric should be two to three times the perimeter of the quilt. Shorter lengths of fabrics can be pieced to make the ruffle this length.

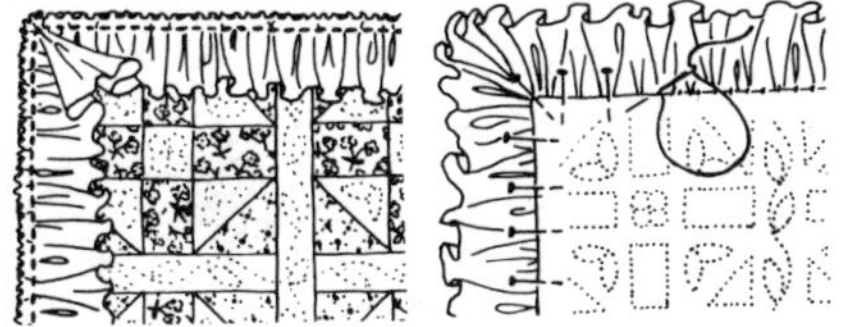

Ruffled Edging

Ruler: a useful tool for measuring. Many quiltmakers prefer a see-through ruler. Some plastic cutting templates also serve as rulers.

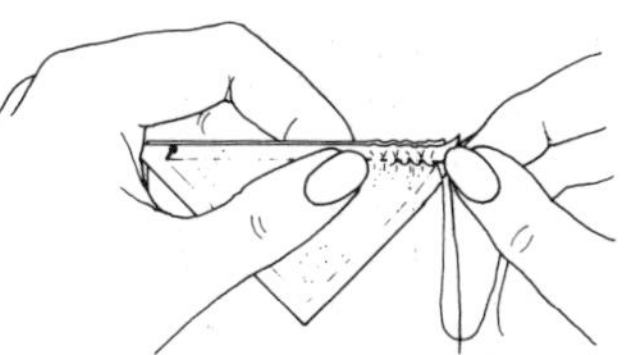

Running Stitch for Hand Piecing

Running Stitch: (1) passing the needle in and out of the fabric along the seam line for hand piecing. The thread color usually matches one or both patches. Running stitches are often about 1/16″.

Running Stitch: (2) passing the needle in and out of the quilt to make even quilting stitches with equal spaces in between.

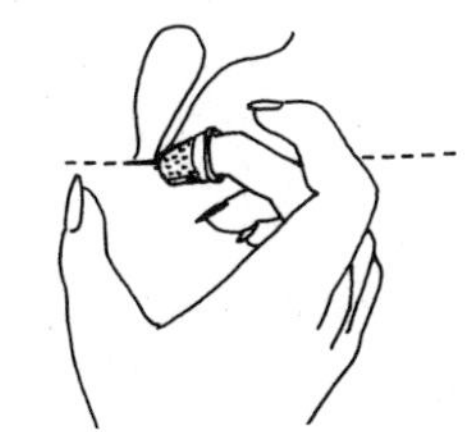

Running Stitch for Hand Quilting

Sampler Quilt
(Diagonal Set With Sashing and Setting Squares)

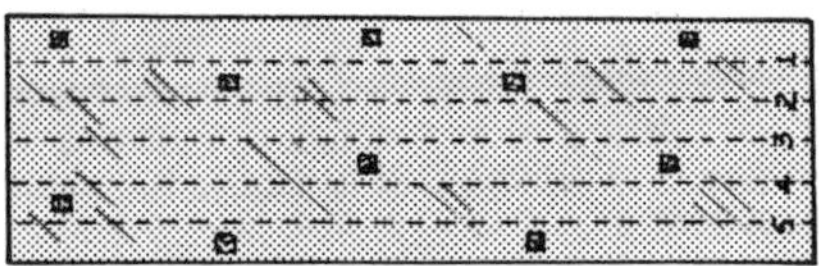

Sandpaper on a Template

A Quilt With Sashing Strips

Safety Pins: items used in a quick method for basting a quilt. Be sure that the safety pins are rustproof and that they will not leave marks in the quilt after they are removed.

Sampler Quilts: quilts made with a different pattern for each block. Sashing (with or without setting squares) is often used in sampler quilts because the sashes unify the varying blocks and also let each block "shine" alone. Sampler blocks can be set diagonally as shown at left, or they can be set in horizontal rows. Sampler quilts are popular with beginners.

Sandpaper: gritty paper (use fine grade) that, when cut into small pieces and attached to rulers and templates, will help prevent slipping while marking and cutting. Some quiltmakers cut templates from sandpaper, but these are not as long-lasting as those that are cut from template plastic.

Sandwich: a word used to describe the layers (or layering) of a quilt.

Sash(ing): strips of fabric sewn between blocks. Sashing separates the blocks, but the visual impact will vary depending on the sash fabric and width. Another name for sashing is lattice stripping.

Sash Width: a dimension that can vary from narrow to wide, perhaps to be even wider than the blocks. Narrow sashes will tend to unify the blocks; wide sashes let each block stand alone and provide areas for quilting motifs.

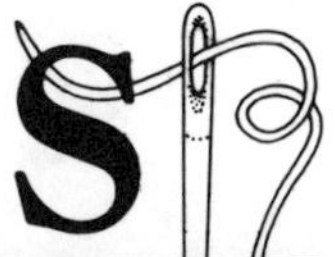

Sashiko: a Japanese style of decorative stitching that is both embroidery and quilting. It is often done with white thread on a dark, solid (such as indigo) background.

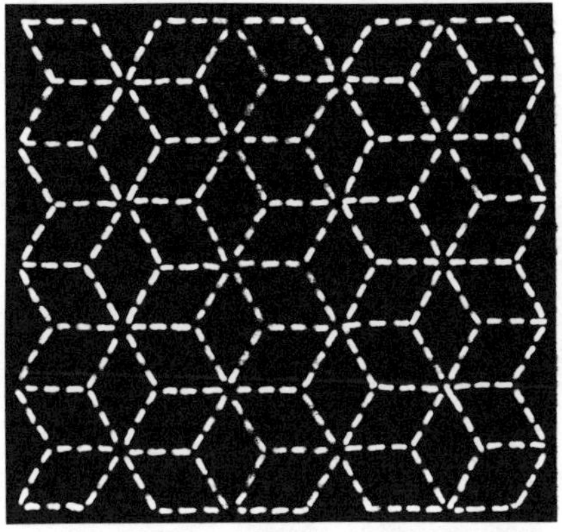
Sashiko

Sashing Seam Allowances: ¼″ allowances that are usually pressed away from the block and toward the sash. When setting squares are used, seam allowances between sashes and setting squares are usually pressed toward the setting square.

Satin Stitch: a decorative embroidery stitch worked by hand to form solid design areas, often on appliquéd picture quilts. Machine appliqué is done with a close zigzag stitch that resembles satin stitch.

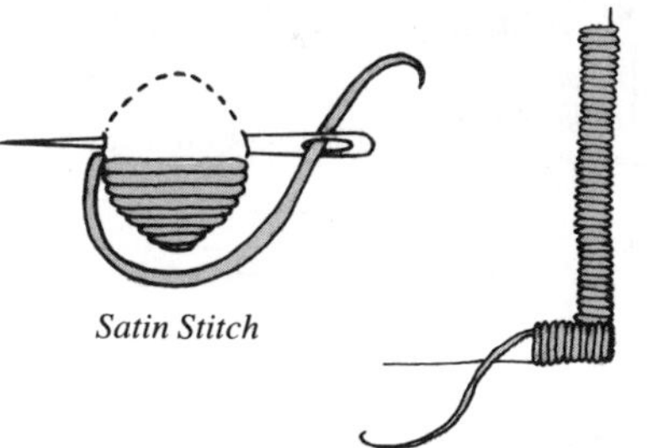
Satin Stitch

Zigzag Stitch for Machine Appliqué

Sawtooth Edging: see Prairie Points.

Scallop Edging: see Clamshell Edging.

Scissors: a necessary tool for quiltmaking. It is important to have special scissors used only for sewing so they will be as sharp as possible. (Cutting paper will dull scissors quickly.) Most quiltmakers enjoy using a pair of dressmaker's shears for cutting patches and a smaller pair of embroidery scissors for clipping threads. Quilters who use a frame often leave their embroidery scissors and thread on the quilt while they work, so they prefer scissors with blunt points that won't accidentally pierce the quilt top.

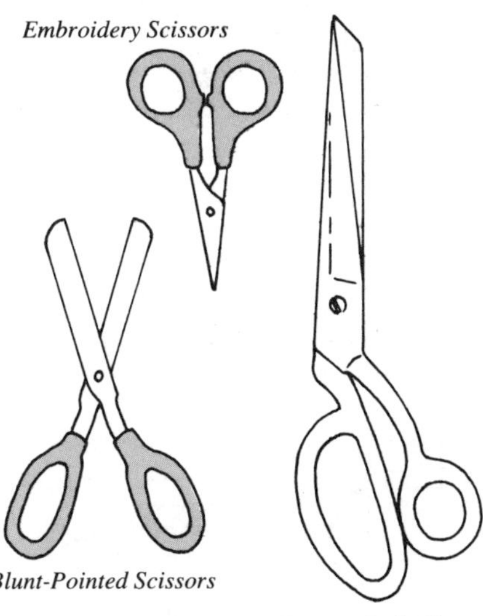
Embroidery Scissors

Blunt-Pointed Scissors

Dressmaker's Shears

Scrap Quilts: those made from col-

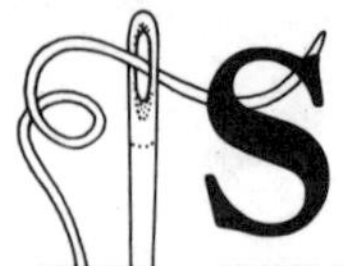

lected fabrics old and new. Scrap quilts frequently use several dozen or even several hundred different fabrics.

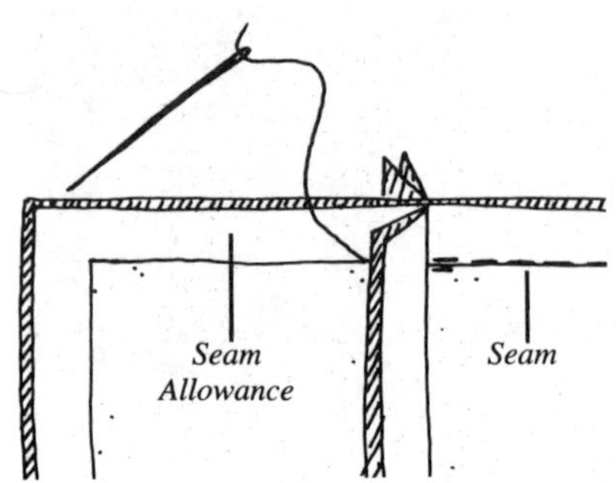

Continuing a Hand-Stitched Seam Through Seam Allowances

Seam: the line of stitching that joins patches or other parts of a quilt.

Seam Allowance: the fabric between the seam line and the cut edge. Seam allowances are usually ¼″ wide; both allowances are most often pressed to one side of the seam, often toward the darker fabric.

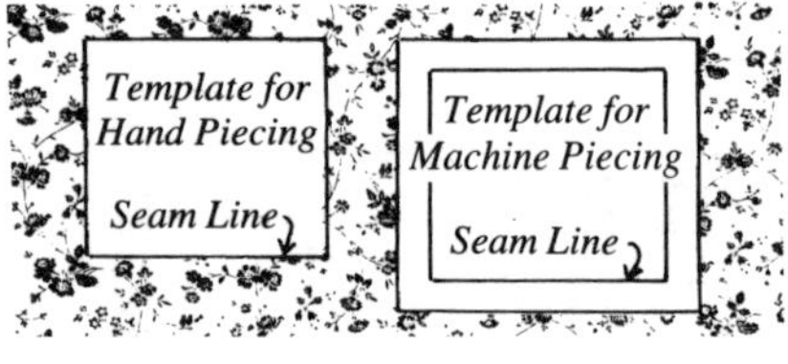

Seam Line: the line, whether marked for hand piecing or unmarked for machine piecing, on which the seam is sewn. When the line is unmarked, the seam is taken ¼″ from the cut edge to leave ¼″-wide seam allowance.

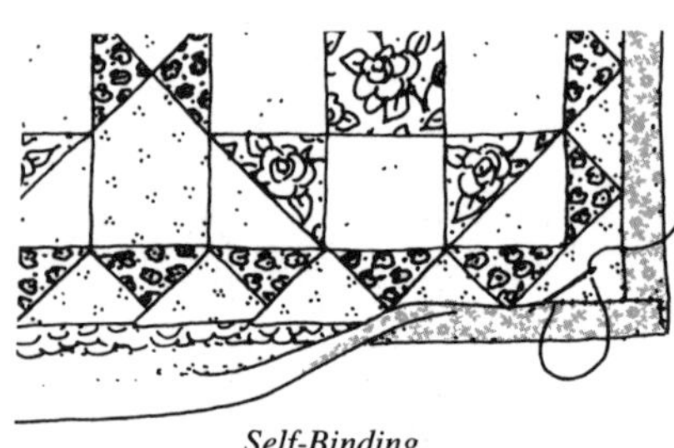
Self-Binding

Self-Binding: an easy edge finish in which the excess lining fabric is rolled around to the front of the quilt, turned under, and blindstitched in place. When making self-binding, be sure to stitch through to the back of the quilt to prevent the batting from shifting.

Selvedges: the lengthwise woven edges of the fabric. Selvedges are more densely woven than the rest of the fabric, causing them to shrink considerably and to be difficult to sew through. Selvedges are removed by cutting away about ½″; they should never be included in border strips. The word is sometimes spelled selvages.

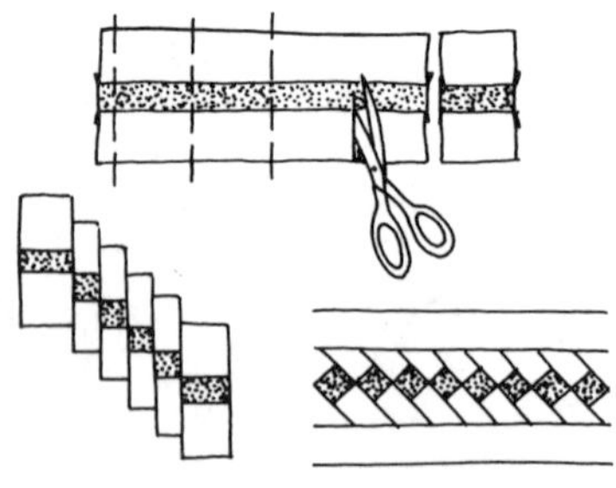
An Example of Seminole Patchwork

Seminole Patchwork: a style of strip piecing used by the Seminole Indians since the 1920s and enjoyed by many quiltmakers today. Strips of fabric (which can be cut quickly using a rotary cutter) are sewn together, then units are cut apart, repositioned, and resewn to form intricate bands of geometric designs suitable for small quilts and for embellishing clothing and household items.

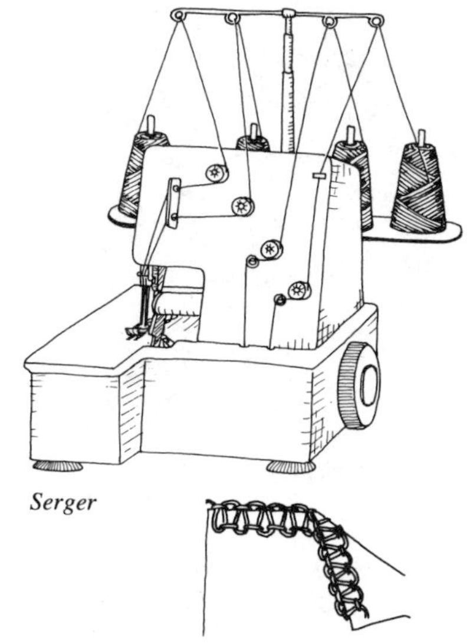

Serger

Stitching Produced by a Serger

Serging: a process of machine stitching a seam and finishing the seam allowances at the same time by using a special machine called a serger. A serger also can be used to finish the edge of a single layer of fabric. Although serging is not frequently used in making quilts, it is useful for related sewing such as making dust ruffles and curtains.

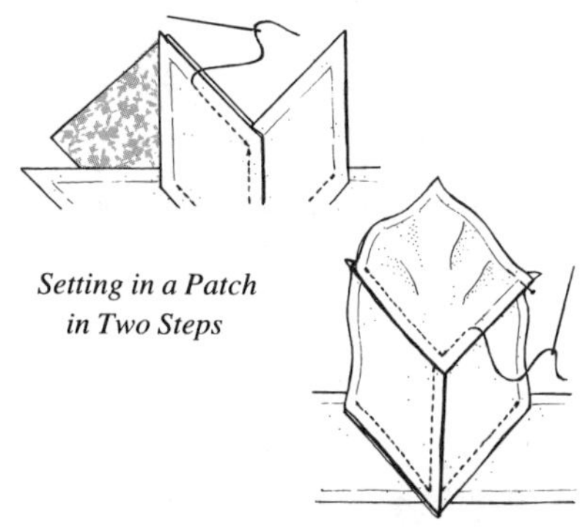

Setting in a Patch in Two Steps

Set-In Seam: a juncture that cannot be sewn in one straight seam. Set-in (or angled) seams are sewn in two steps: first one side of the angled patch or unit is sewn, then the other side. Beginning quiltmakers may want to avoid set-in seams until they are comfortable sewing straight seams with accuracy.

Set(ting): the arrangement of blocks and other components. Sets are usually either horizontal or diagonal, depending on the block orientation.

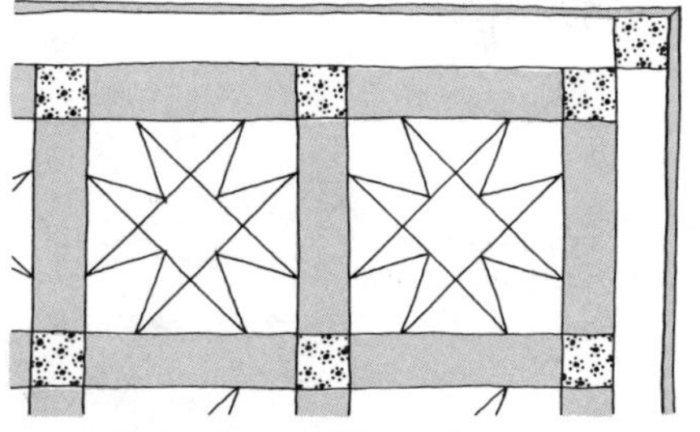

Setting Squares With Sashing

Setting Squares: squares of fabric sewn at the block intersections and used with sashing. Setting squares can help the blocks lose their individuality to create designs within the overall repeat pattern of the quilt.

Sewing Machine: an optional tool for

S

quiltmaking. Quilts were made entirely by hand for hundreds of years, but the invention of the sewing machine in the mid-1800s changed that. Today many quiltmakers work by machine for some or all of the steps in quiltmaking.

Appliqué Patches Are Sewn From Lower Layer to Upper Layer

Sewing Order: for appliqué, the sequence in which patches are added to the background. Some blocks have no overlapping patches, so the order of stitching is not important. Other blocks have layer upon layer of patches. Sew the patches from the lowest layer to the uppermost layer. For piecing, the sequence in which patches are sewn together. This sequence is indicated in blown-apart piecing diagrams.

Block-Piecing Diagram: Patches are Sewn in Units, Then Units are Joined

Shade: a variation of a color that has had black added to it; a darker version of a hue.

Shadow Appliqué: a technique of placing colored fabric shapes on a background and quilting through translucent fabric (such as organza) around them. Because the organza lightens the color of the underneath patch, bright colors are usually used.

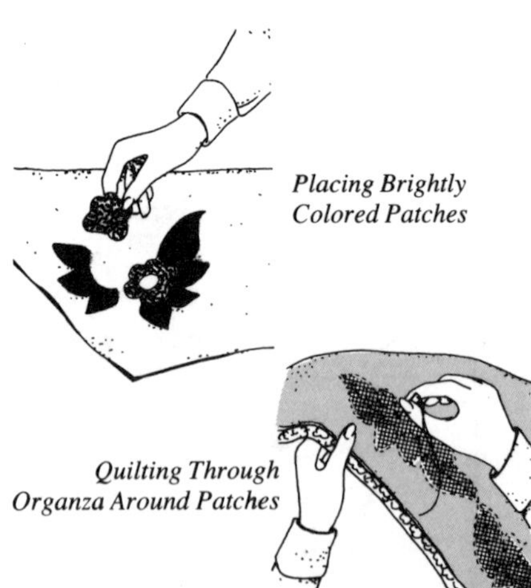

Placing Brightly Colored Patches

Quilting Through Organza Around Patches

Shadow Appliqué

Sharp: a needle, longer than a between, with a small eye. Sharps are excellent needles for hand appliqué. Their length allows a comfortable grip; the narrow shaft slides easily through the appliqué patch and background.

Shrinkage: the reduction in the size of fabric when it is washed and dried; also, the change in size of a quilt when it is quilted. Fabric will shrink up to 8

percent when it is washed and dried; quilts can be several inches (or more) smaller after the tops are quilted. Finished quilt sizes listed for patterns in books and magazines do not take this after-quilting shrinkage into consideration.

Mark Signature on Tracing Paper, Embroider Through Paper, Then Tear Away the Paper

A Label Made With Permanent Ink

Examples of Signatures

Signature: an important final step in quiltmaking. The signature can be done on the quilt's front or back, in embroidery or with a permanent fabric marker or india ink. Add a date and other information such as the name of the recipient or the city and state. Future owners of the quilt will be very grateful for these efforts.

Simple Sashing

Simple Sashing: plain sashing strips that do not have setting squares to break them up. Simple sashing has short lengths between blocks for the horizontal or diagonal rows and long lengths between rows.

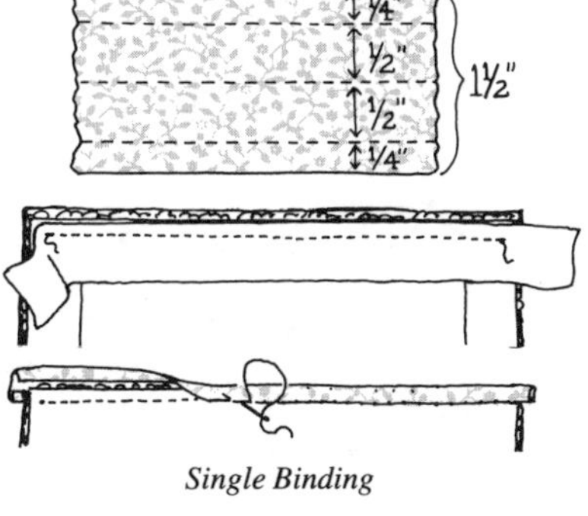

Single Binding

Single Binding: binding that finishes with one layer of fabric. Single binding is cut two times the finished width plus two seam allowances (often about 1½" total). It is applied right side down on the front side of the quilt using either individual strips or continuous binding. After stitching it in place, fold the binding to the back of the quilt, turn under the allowance, and blindstitch the fold so that the binding just covers the stitching.

Attaching a Sleeve Before Binding the Quilt

Sleeve: a tube of fabric sewn to the top back side (and sometimes the bottom) of a quilt to accommodate a pole for hanging the quilt. Sleeves can be made

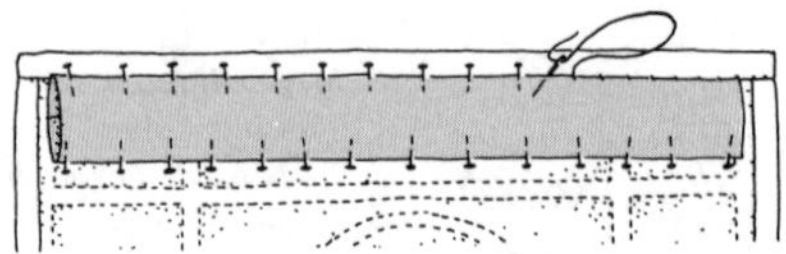
Attaching a Sleeve After the Quilt is Finished

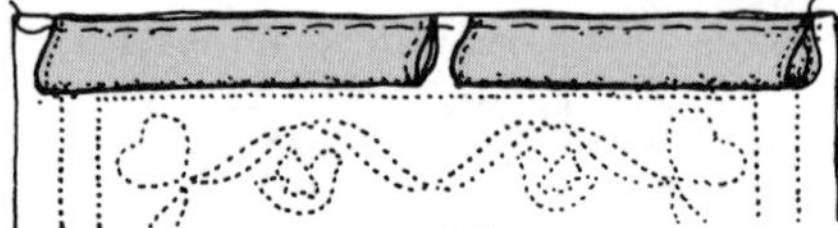
Two Short Sleeves to Accommodate a Bracket

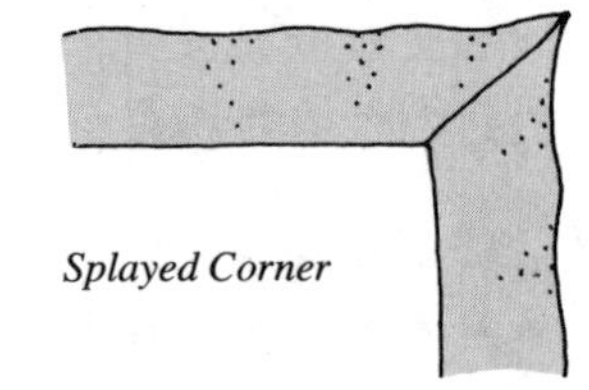
Splayed Corner

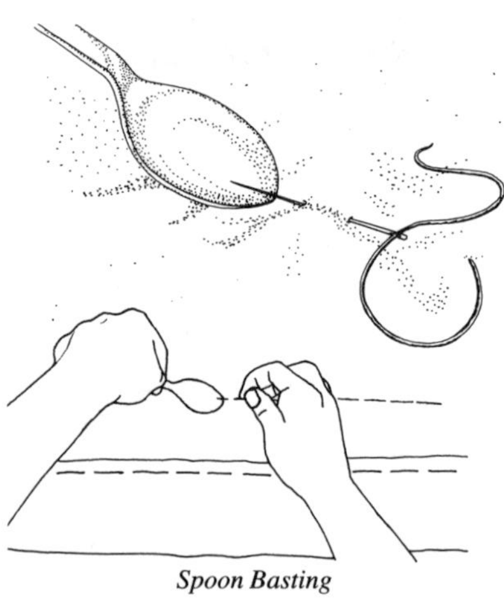
Spoon Basting

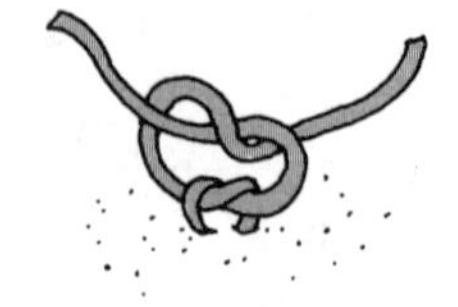
Square Knot

of fabric that matches the lining or they can be made of contrasting fabric. The tube should measure about 2″ (made from a 5″-wide strip of fabric with a ½″ seam) if a sash curtain rod will be used for hanging; it should finish at least 4″ (made from a 9″-wide strip of fabric with a ½″ seam) if a wooden closet rod or heavy curtain rod will be used. Large quilts will need a support bracket in the center, so two short sleeves should be sewn side by side with a gap for the bracket. Quilts to be sent to shows should always include a sleeve that is at least 4″ wide.

Splayed Corners: those that appear stretched and don't create a 90° angle. This problem usually is caused by marking miters inaccurately or by stretching the mitered seam, and it may be aggravated by flared borders.

Spoon Basting: catching the point of the needle with a spoon when basting. The needle is held in one hand while basting, the spoon is held in the other. (Both hands are above the quilt.) Catching the needle with a spoon this way prevents the point from snagging the quilt top and may help the basting process go more quickly. (Use an old spoon since it will likely get scratched by the needle.)

Square Knot: the best knot for tying a quilt. To make a square knot, hold one "tail" in each hand. Wrap the left tail over the right tail, pull tightly, then wrap the new right tail over the new left tail and tighten the knot. Clip the thread or yarn to leave tails about ¾″-1½″.

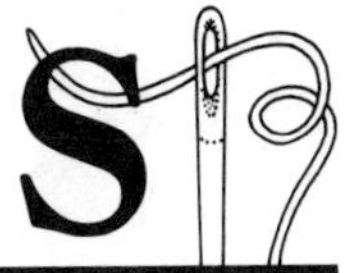

Stab Stitch: quilting that is done one stitch at a time by poking the needle straight down or straight up through the quilt.

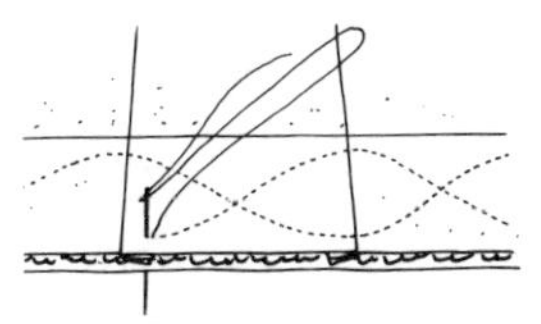

Stab Stitching

Stained-Glass Appliqué: a design style, which imitates the look of stained glass, where black bias stripping is appliquéd over the edges of patches. Patterns for stained glass are easily adapted to stained-glass appliqué.

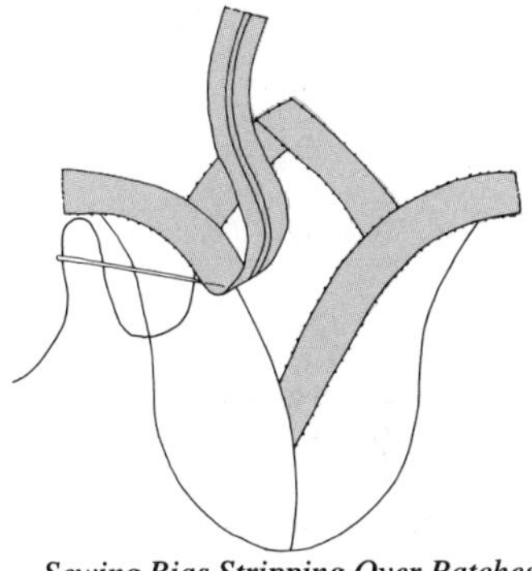

Sewing Bias Stripping Over Patches for Stained-Glass Appliqué

Stencil: a cut-out pattern through which designs can be marked for quilting or painted for stenciling. Stencils often are made from lightweight cardboard or plastic.

Stenciling: a technique for painting on fabric by dabbing a special paintbrush over a cut-out stencil. Freezer paper, with the to-be-stenciled shape(s) cut away, can be ironed on the fabric. After applying paint, the freezer paper can be peeled away and reused. Stenciling is much faster than appliqué with similar results.

Stenciling on Fabric With a Freezer-Paper Stencil

Stipple Quilting: that which moves in close meandering lines to heavily quilt an area of a quilt. These quilting lines usually don't cross each other. Most often such quilting serves to contrast with unquilted areas that will be noticeably puffy by comparison.

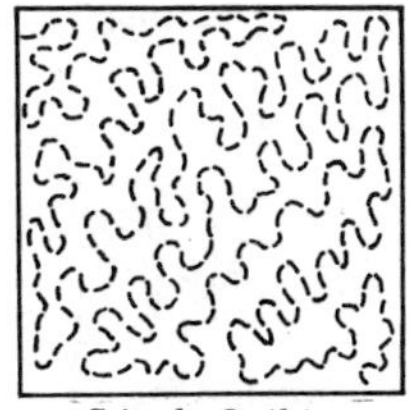

Stipple Quilting

Stitches Per Inch: the number of quilting stitches that can be worked per inch; they are counted on one side of the quilt, usually the top. Beginners might achieve only three or four stitches per inch; experienced quilters can

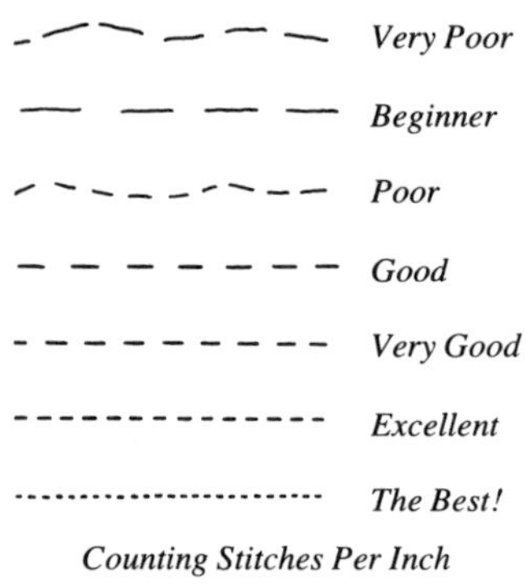

Counting Stitches Per Inch

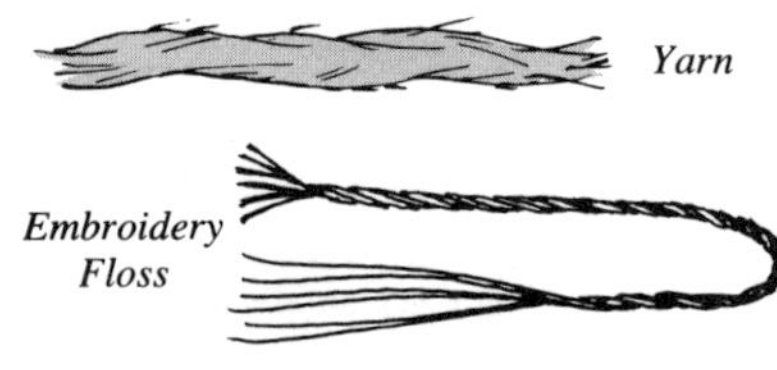

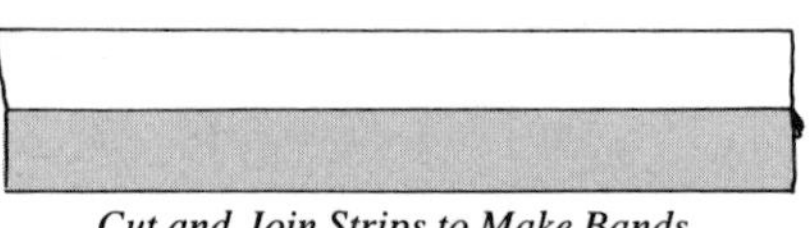
Cut and Join Strips to Make Bands

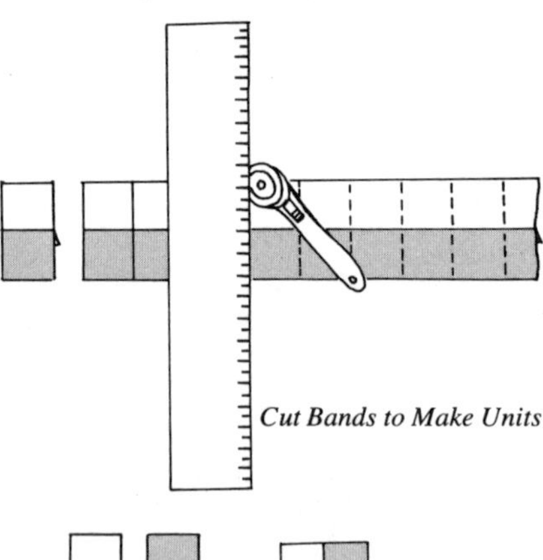

Strip Piecing

sometimes get 15 or even 20 stitches per inch. The thickness of the batting is a significant determining factor in the size and spacing of quilting stitches.

Story Quilts: those that depict an event, whether real or imaginary. See Picture Quilts.

Straight-Grain Binding: stripping cut on either crosswise or lengthwise grain. Straight grain has very little (if any) stretch. Straight-grain strips can be cut in any length (if you are willing to purchase sufficient yardage). Often binding is cut from the same fabric as borders and, therefore, it will not require the purchase of any additional fabric if binding is cut alongside border strips.

Strand: a thread or single yarn that can be used individually. Embroidery floss has six strands, which can be separated and used individually or in any number.

String Quilts: those made from very narrow strips of fabric, often in random or varying widths. String quilts are associated with frugality, but the style certainly can be chosen for its graphic qualities. String-quilt blocks often are made with a foundation fabric to stabilize the small pieces of fabric.

Strip Piecing: a technique that became very popular in the 1980s for its speed. Strips of fabric are cut (usually with a rotary cutter) and joined to make bands; the bands are cut into units and the units are assembled to make blocks.

Striped Fabric for Binding: printed

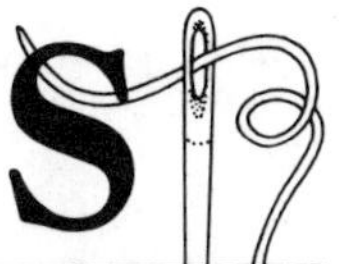

or woven stripes that can create special binding effects. When cut on straight grain, the stripes will frame the quilt. If bias is your choice, the stripes will appear to twirl. Striped fabric will require careful cutting and matching to achieve pleasing results.

Binding With Bias-Cut Fabric

Striped Fabric for Sashing: a design that can be very effective if setting squares are used. For simple sashing, striped fabric may not be as successful as a solid or print because the stripes will stop abruptly at the intersections.

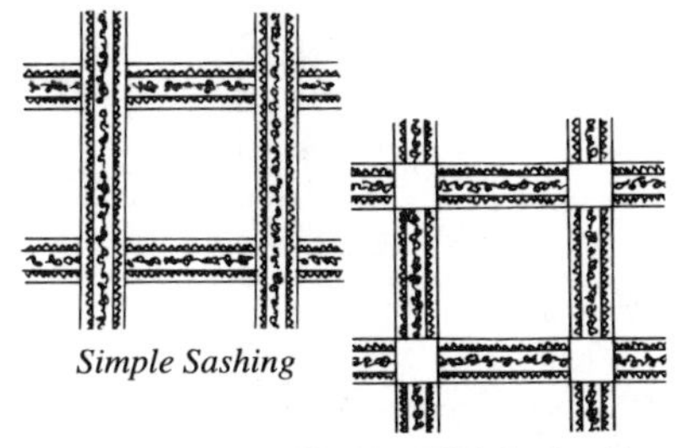

Simple Sashing

Sashing With Setting Squares

Strippie Quilts: those that have vertical bands of simple piecing that alternate with long sashing.

An Example of a Strippie Quilt

Stuffed Quilting: see Trapunto.

Summer Quilt (or Spread): that which has no batting, making it lighter for sleeping in hot weather.

Surface Knot: a knot made at the end of a length of quilting thread right on the surface of the quilt top. To make the knot rest on the surface, hold it under a finger as the thread tightens. Then insert the needle through the exact hole where it came out to pop the knot into the quilt batting. Take an inch-long stitch through the batting, bring the needle back through the quilt top, then clip the thread at the surface to leave the knot and tail inside the quilt.

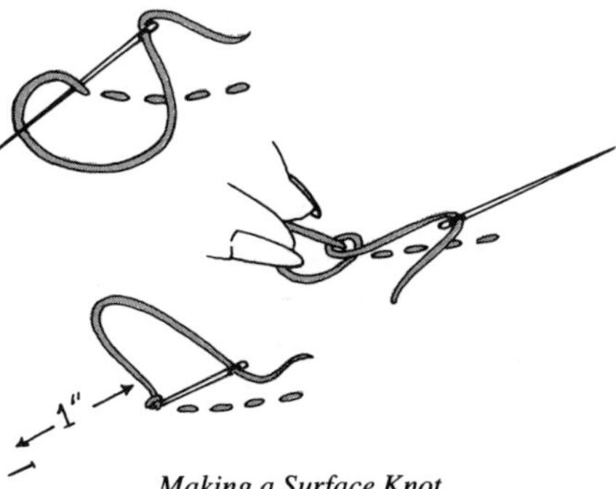

Making a Surface Knot

Symmetry: balance achieved by mirror (exact, yet reversed) images or balanced proportions even if the design is not exactly the same on both halves.

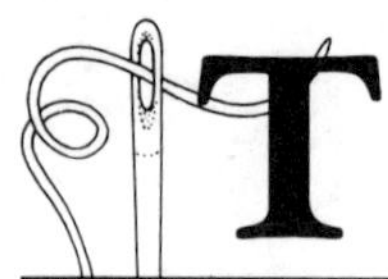

T

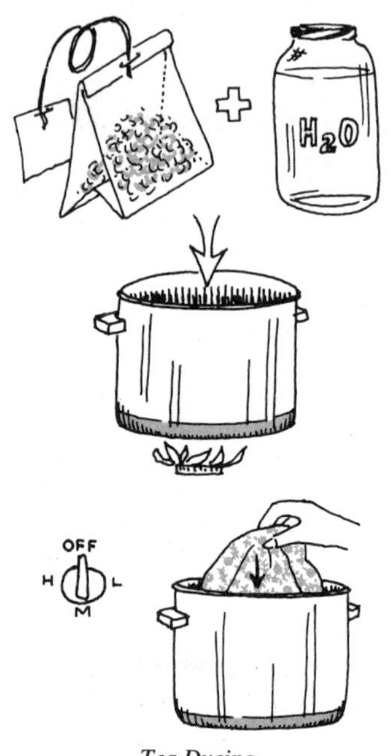

Tea Dyeing

Tearing Fabric

Marking Around a Template

Tea Dyeing: an easy way to give fabrics a slight brown tint or an antique look that is especially effective on bright white fabrics and light prints. Fabric should be rinsed in hot water before dyeing. Steep a family size tea bag in a quart of boiling water; let fabric soak in the tea until the desired shade is obtained. Adjust the amount of water, number of tea bags, and soaking time as necessary to achieve the desired effect and accommodate the piece(s) of fabric.

Tearing Fabric: ripping material on crosswise or lengthwise grain. Tearing is not recommended because it can stretch the fabric and can cause the threads to "run."

Template: the pattern around which seam lines or cutting lines are marked on the fabric. Templates can be the paper pattern, but more often they are made from see-through plastic, which will last indefinitely. Cardboard and sandpaper also are used to make templates. Templates for machine piecing include seam allowances; those for hand piecing do not. Mark the patch letter and grain-line arrow on the template. Short sashes and setting squares are cut from templates; long sashes are cut with a rotary cutter or scissors on lines that have been marked with a yardstick and pencil.

Tension: a term referring to the tightness of the two threads on a sewing machine and the resulting line of stitching. When the tension is balanced, the threads will lock between the fabrics and not on the surface of either piece. Usually an adjustment of the upper tension only will be sufficient to correct an imbalance; the bobbin tension usually can remain the same. Tension often must be adjusted for machine quilting. When adjusting tension, practice first on fabrics (with batting if simulating machine quilting) to check the adjustment before working on the quilt.

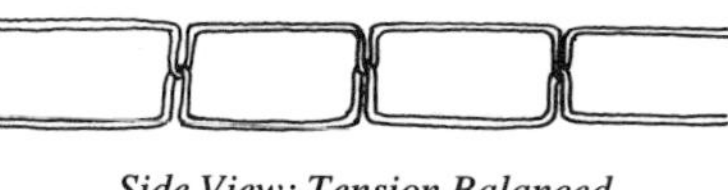

Side View: Tension Balanced

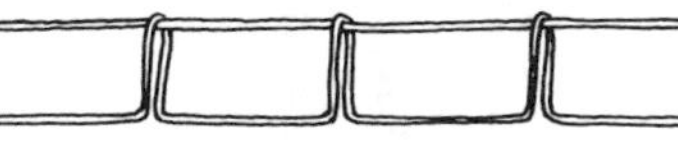

Top Thread Too Tight or Bobbin Thread Too Loose

Top Thread Too Loose or Bobbin Thread Too Tight

Thimble: a metal or leather device worn on the sewing finger to protect it. For hand quilting, it is preferable that the thimble have indentations to help guide the needle and prevent it from slipping.

Metal Thimble With a Rounded Top

Metal Thimble With a Recessed Top

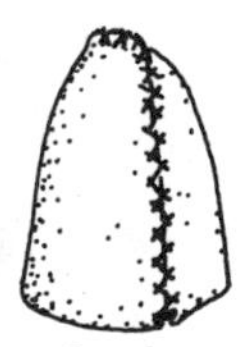

Leather Thimble

Thread: the strand pulled through fabric to hold a quilt together. It is available in many qualities and virtually every color imaginable. Good thread is a joy to use; bad thread can be a nightmare. See also Quilting Thread.

Thread Color: for hand appliqué, the color of thread should match the fabric patch being applied (not the background). When binding a quilt, match the thread to the binding fabric. For machine appliqué, the thread can match the patch or it can contrast for stronger definition of shapes. For piecing, the thread ideally should match one or both fabrics. When a choice is practical, match the darker fabric. If matching the fabric would require changing the thread in the sewing machine too many times to keep your patience intact, select a medium neutral color such as gray or beige.

Thread

T

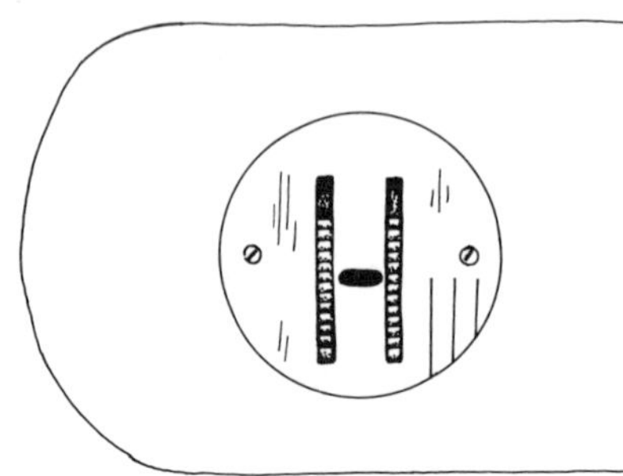

Throat Plate

Throat Plate: the surface of the sewing machine where the actual stitching happens. See also Feed Dogs.

Throw: a small quilt for cuddling up with a good book or in front of the television. A throw is the quilted version of an afghan.

A Throw in Use

Tifaifai: Tahitian pieced or appliquéd bedcovers, which are not quilted and do not have batting. Often they are made by groups and may be given as a ceremonial gift.

Tint: a variation of a color that has had white added to it; a lighter version of a hue.

Top: the upper layer of a quilt, which has the design and is usually the side that is seen.

Topper: a quilt used on the top of a bed over a bedspread or larger quilt. Toppers also can be used as throws.

An Example of a Topper

Traditional Quilts: those made from time-honored designs that typically use repeated blocks.

Transfer: to mark a design in some way other than free-hand drawing. Methods include iron-on commercial transfers, ironing on a photocopy, tracing over a light box, and using a transfer pencil.

Trapunto: insertion of stuffing or yarn between layers of a quilt (after quilting) to give high relief and texture. Trapunto shows up best on solid

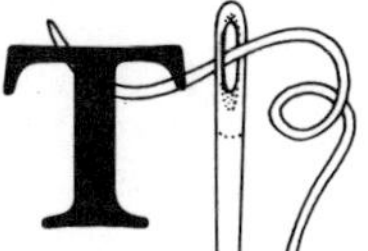

fabrics. Trapunto is easily accomplished by using a 6″-long yarn or trapunto needle to insert fluffy yarn from the lining side of the quilt.

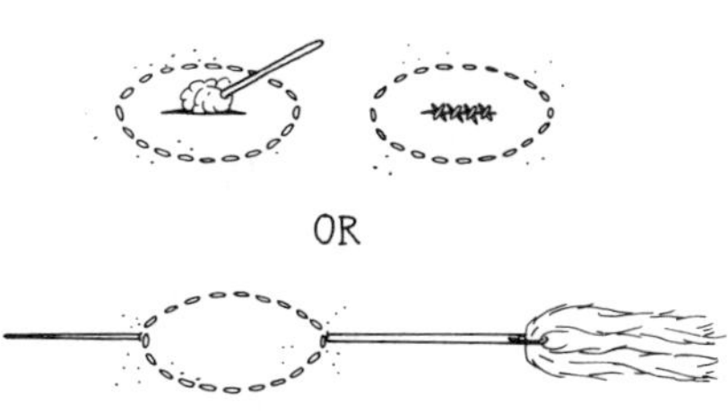

Trapunto

Trimming Behind Patches: cutting away the background fabric or underneath appliqué patches to leave only one layer of fabric. Leave 3⁄16″ to 1⁄4″ allowance on the back side. Such trimming sometimes cuts through previous stitching, in which case additional backstitches should be made to secure the patch.

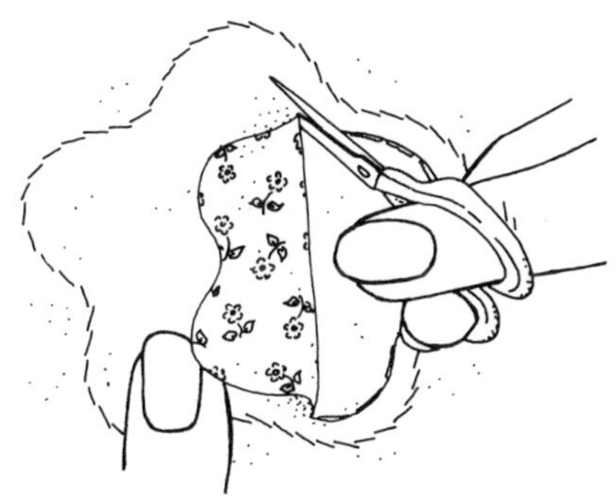
Trimming Behind an Appliqué Patch

Tufting: see Tying.

Turkey Red: a color of cloth and type of dye that became known in the 19th century for its reliable colorfastness.

Turn-Under Allowance: the amount of fabric outside the turn-under line for folding under to leave a crisp, folded edge in hand appliqué. (Satin-stitched machine-appliqué patches usually are not turned under and thus require no turn-under allowances.) Turn-under allowances usually are 3⁄16″ wide.

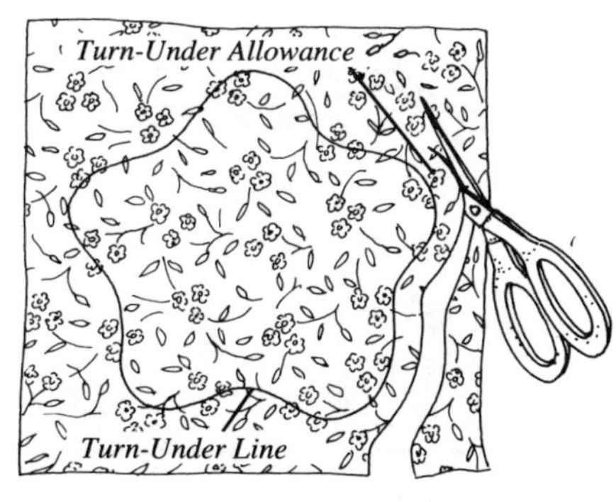

Turn-Under Lines: the markings made around a template on the right side of the fabric to indicate the finished edge of an appliqué patch. When properly appliquéd with blind stitch, the turn-under line should be tucked just out of sight. Cutting lines for hand appliqué are judged "by eye" 3⁄16″ outside the marked turn-under lines.

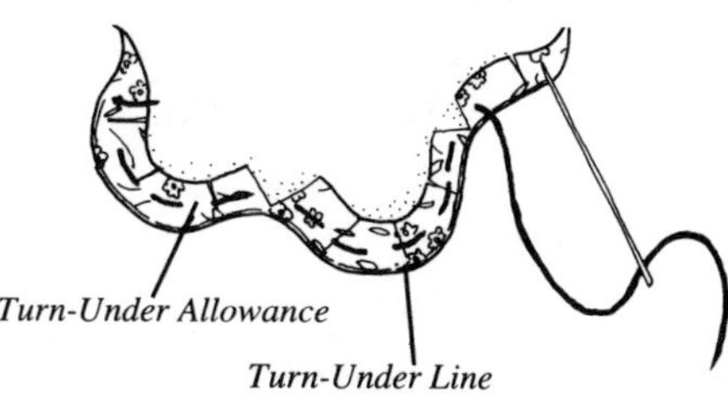

Turning Under Corners on Appliqués: one useful method for achieving

T

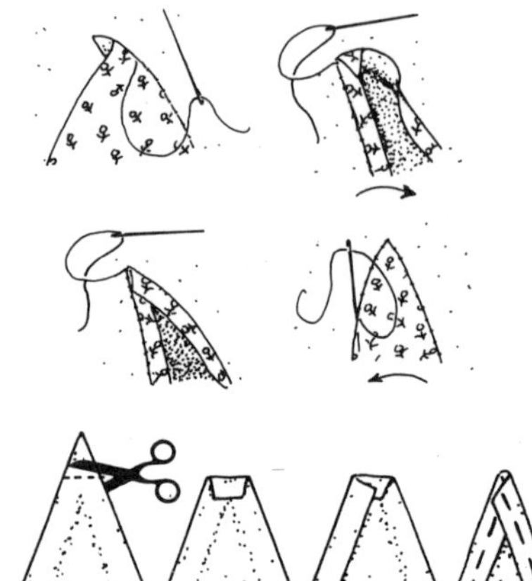

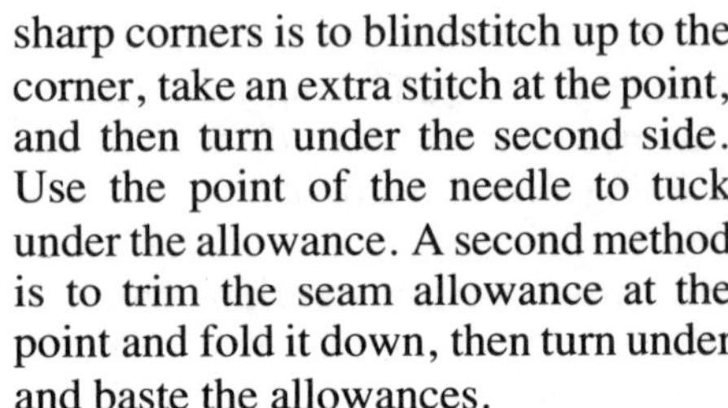

sharp corners is to blindstitch up to the corner, take an extra stitch at the point, and then turn under the second side. Use the point of the needle to tuck under the allowance. A second method is to trim the seam allowance at the point and fold it down, then turn under and baste the allowances.

Turning Under Corners on Appliqués

Twin Bed: mattress size is 39″ x 75″.

Two-Block Quilt: one made from two block designs that alternate. Such quilts often use two blocks that share some major seams, thus creating a blended design.

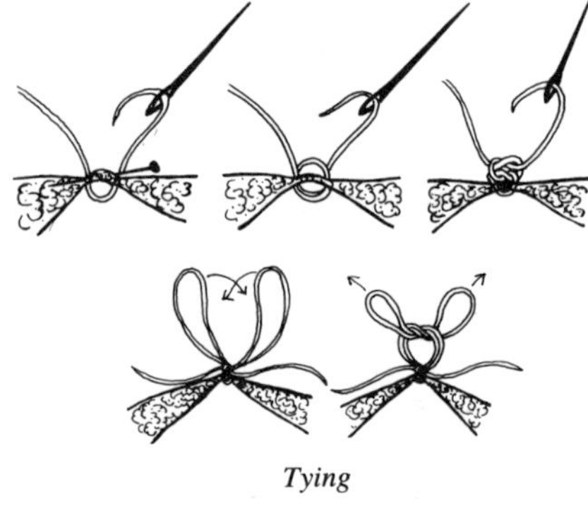

Tying

Two-Sided Quilt: a term referring to a quilt that has piecing or appliqué on both sides of a quilt. Often one side is more elaborate than the other.

Tying: fastening the layers of the quilt with yarn, pearl cotton, embroidery floss, or narrow ribbon with individual tied knots or bows. The tails for ties can be on the front of the quilt or the back. Square knots usually are used to tie quilts. See also Methodist Knotting.

U

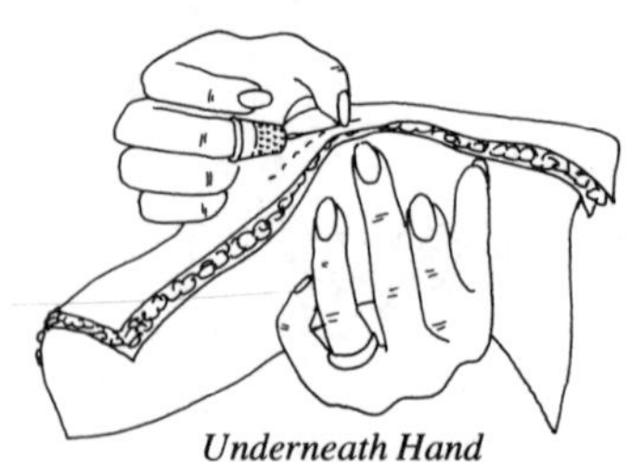

Underneath Hand

Underneath Hand: the hand that is held under a quilt while hand quilting and which feels the prick of the needle. Right-handers would use their left hand under the quilt; left-handers would hold the quilt with the right hand underneath. Some quiltmakers protect the pricked finger with tape or a

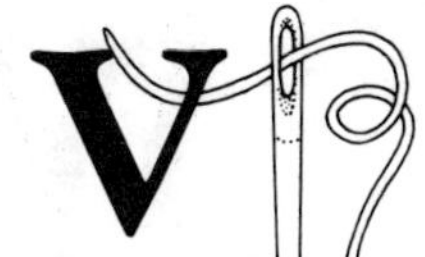

thimble; other quilters prefer to build up a callus in order to feel and guide the needle.

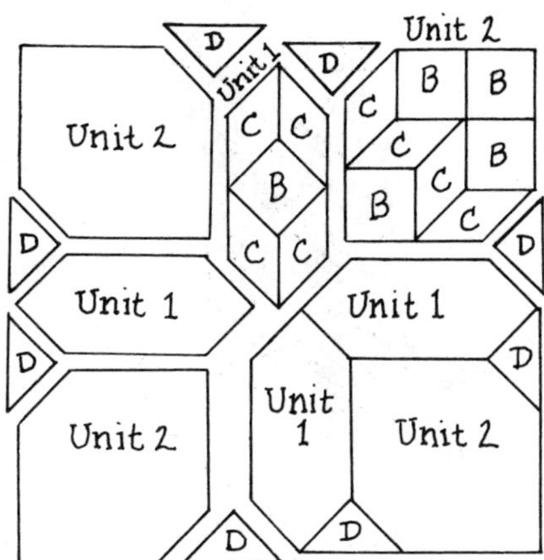

Piecing Diagram With Units

Unit: a portion of a block or border, which is usually indicated by a piecing diagram to guide the quiltmaker in construction.

Unroll: to remove a batting from its package and allow it to lie flat so that the wrinkles will relax before assembling the layers of the quilt.

Utility Quilts: those made for warmth and practical use without extravagance in materials or labor.

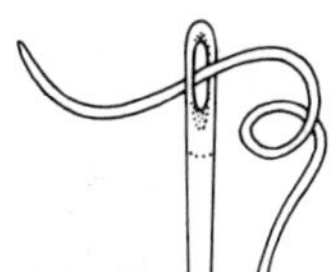

Value: a term used to express the lightness or darkness of a color.

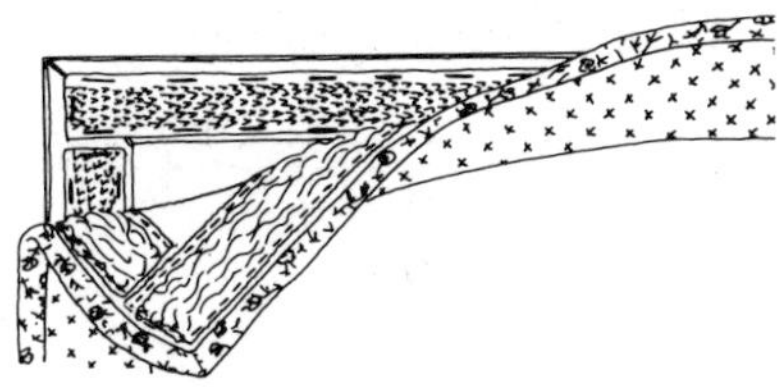

Hanging a Quilt With Velcro™

Velcro™: a two-part tape (one part has hooks; the other part has loops) used for closures on sewing projects and for hanging quilts on a wall. When hanging quilts with Velcro™, sew one tape to the upper back side of the quilt and staple the other tape to a wooden strip that can be mounted on the wall. Press the two tapes together.

Vertical Row of Blocks

Vertical Row: a row of blocks, with or without sashing, that runs from the top of the quilt to the bottom. Most quilts are constructed in horizontal rows, but some designs are better suited to assembly in vertical rows or columns.

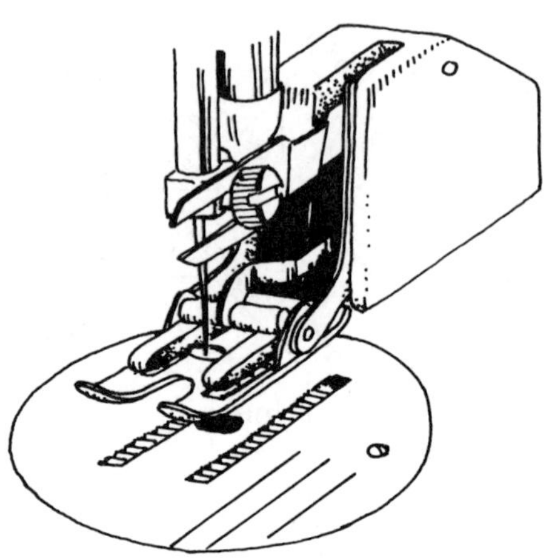

A Walking Foot
(Used in Place of a Regular Presser Foot)

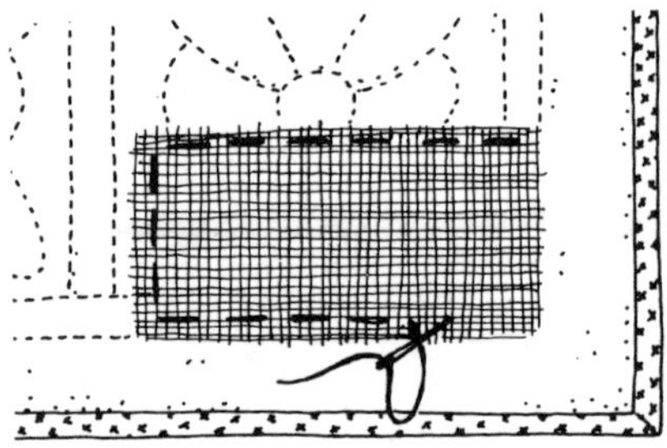

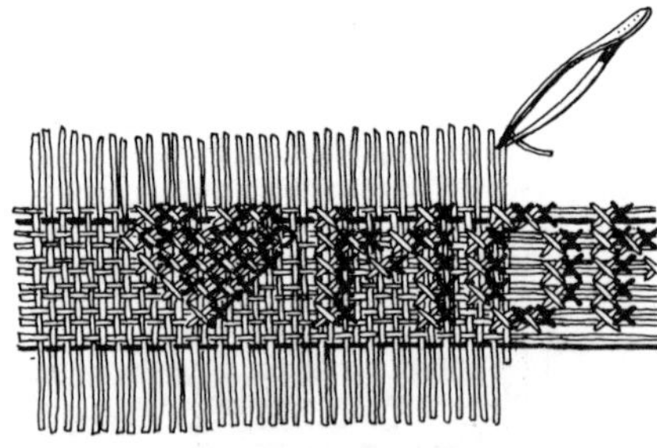

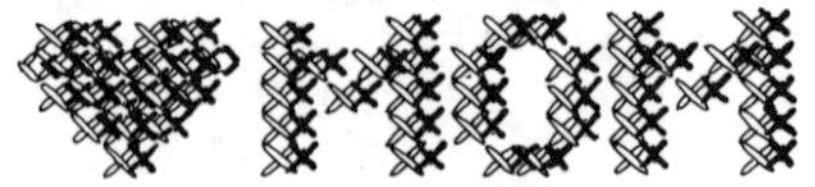

Cross Stitch Over Waste Canvas

Wadding: see Batting.

Walking Foot: a sewing machine attachment that replaces the regular presser foot for machine quilting. A walking foot feeds a quilt more evenly than the regular presser foot does; it is well worth the investment for anyone doing much machine quilting.

Warp: the threads that are parallel to the fabric selvedges; lengthwise grain. Warp threads have very little, if any, stretch.

Waste Canvas: very useful material for doing embroidered inscriptions with cross stitches counted from a chart. Waste canvas resembles penelope needlepoint canvas, except that every tenth thread is blue for easy counting. It is basted on fabric or to a quilt, the embroidery is done over the canvas threads, and then the canvas is soaked in water to release the starch. Canvas threads are then pulled out with tweezers to leave perfect embroidery without markings.

Water-Erasable Marking Pen: a tool for marking quilting lines that was an invention of the 1980s. Also called "spit pens," these markers have received mixed reviews because of their unpredictable lasting quality. In humid climates, the markings can disappear too soon; in other circumstances the marks can be difficult to remove. Markings can actually be permanently set if they are accidentally ironed. Test any marker, but these in particular, before use on a quilt.

Waterbed Quilts: due to variations in styles of beds, quilts made for waterbeds should be planned after measuring the bed. Some waterbed quilts are tucked between the mattress and supporting rails; others are made to go over the rail as on a regular bed.

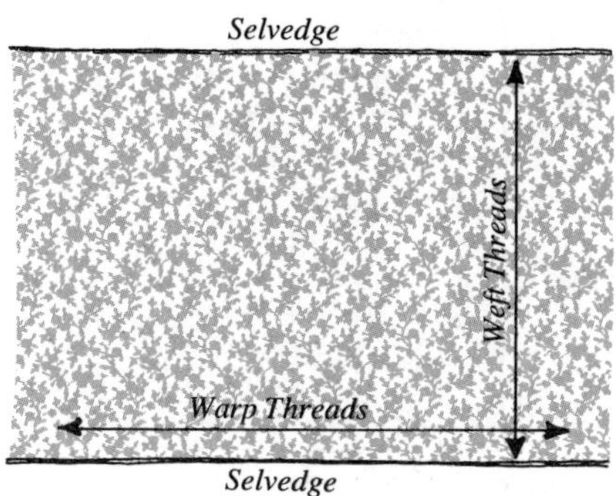

Weft: the threads that are perpendicular to the fabric selvedges; crosswise grain. Weft threads may have some stretch.

White-On-White Quilts: whole-cloth quilts that are white or off-white.

Whole-Cloth Quilts: those made from one large (perhaps seamed) piece of fabric that is usually a solid color. Whole-cloth quilts feature the quilting as the primary design element.

An Example of a White-on-White or Whole-Cloth Quilt

Width of Borders: the cut dimension of border strips, which should include the finished width plus seam allowances.

Wool Batting: batting that is made from wool. Wool batting is not bonded (but is sometimes needlepunched) and will usually require close quilting. It has natural lanolin (unless the fiber has been well-washed) and good body. Sometimes wool batting is encased in cheesecloth to minimize bearding of the fibers. Use wool batting only in quilts that will not be washed or those that will be washed by soaking (without agitation) and rinsing in cool water. Avoid drastic changes in the water temperature, which will shrink wool fiber.

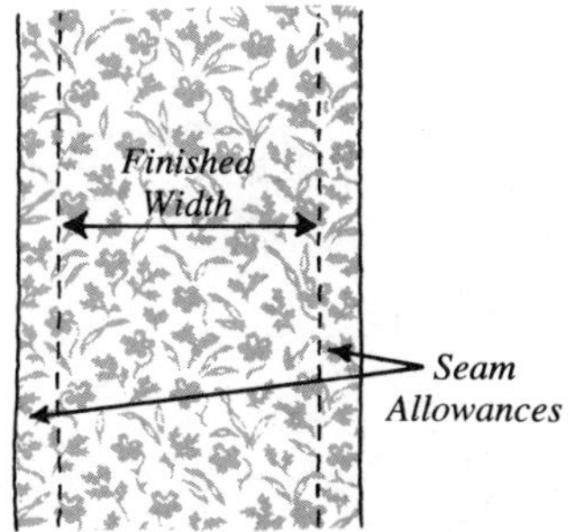

Border Width (Finished Width Plus Seam Allowances)

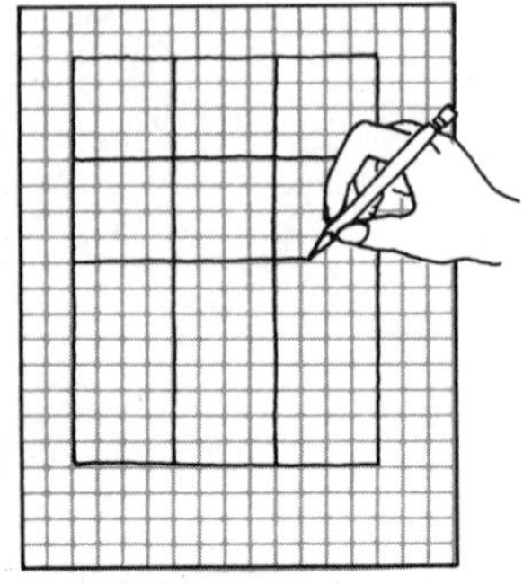

Work Sheet for a Quilt Design

Work Sheet: the plan for a quilt, drawn to scale on graph paper. The squares on the paper can be counted to determine the correct sizes for block patches, sashing, and setting squares. It is easiest to use paper with one square equaling one inch of the quilt. Of course, you will need to add seam allowances to the finished dimensions before cutting patches. One easy way to change the size of a quilt is to change the scale of the graph paper (having one square equal ¾″ or 1½″, for example).

Photocopies of Work Sheets for Coloring

Work Sheet Photocopies: copies of intermediate and final quilt plans that are very useful for design options and coloring fun. Many quiltmakers who have access to a photocopy machine record their design ideas along the way to build a collection of work sheets. Once you have chosen your favorite quilt plan, make several photocopies to color with pens or pencils.

Writing on Fabric: inscribing or signing a patch or a quilt with permanent ink. Select a marker intended for use on fabric and test it for permanence. Fabric can be stabilized by pressing freezer paper to the wrong side. Masking tape can be used to indicate lines on which to write. After writing, peel away the freezer paper and tape.

Wrong Side of Fabric

Wrong Side of Fabric: the back side, which for a print is usually lighter and more blurry than the right side. (Solid fabric does not have right and wrong sides.) Sometimes the wrong side of the fabric may be used as part of the quilt design, especially for picture quilts.

X-Ray Film: a good material to use for making templates.

Xerography: the process of photocopying. Photocopying will distort the image size, making the process unadvisable for reproducing patterns if accuracy is important (as it is for pieced quilt designs). Photocopying may be an infringement of copyright. The process can also be used to make iron-on transfers, but the image will be reversed from that of the original. Use fresh (no more than two-hours old) photocopies for the best transfers.

A Quiltmaker's X-Ray Film

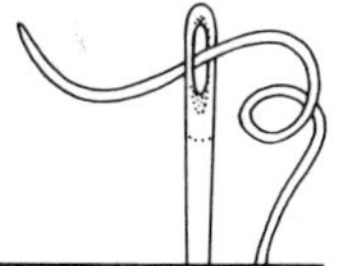

Yard Goods: see Fabric.

Yardage: a term referring to a quantity of fabric. Yardage requirements are listed with most quilt patterns; many quiltmakers choose to buy extra fabric to ensure having plenty for a project and to add to their collections. The cotton fabrics favored by quiltmakers are usually 44″ to 45″ wide before shrinking. Most quilt shops sell fabric in ⅛-yard increments. Many also sell pieces in half width; see Fat Eighth, Fat Quarter, and Long Half.

Yarn Needle: a long, thick needle with a big eye used for tying quilts and doing trapunto. Select a needle just big enough to accommodate the yarn since a too-big needle will leave holes in the quilt and will be difficult to pull through.

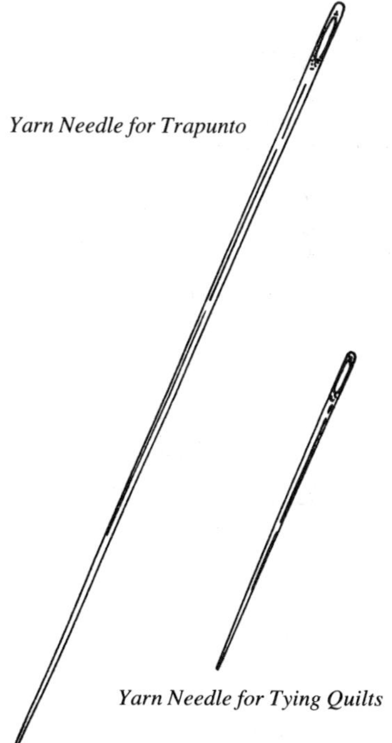

Yarn Needle for Trapunto

Yarn Needle for Tying Quilts

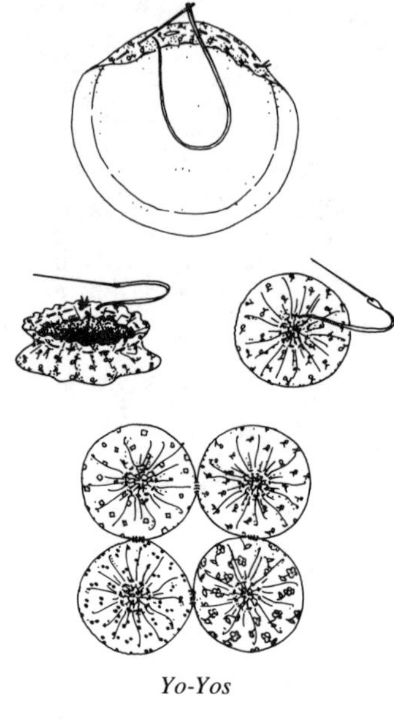

Yo-Yos

Youth Bed: mattress size is 33″ x 66″.

Yo-Yo Quilts: decorative bedcovers that are made of circles of fabric without batting or lining. Each yo-yo is made from a fabric circle cut approximately twice the size of the finished yo-yo. The edge is turned under to the wrong side with a running stitch, then the thread is pulled to gather the circle. Finished yo-yos are joined with overcast stitches. Another name for yo-yos is Suffolk puffs.

Yukata: Japanese cotton fabric, used to make summer kimonos, that can be incorporated in quiltmaking. It is narrow in width (about 14″), and the design is identical on both sides of the fabric.

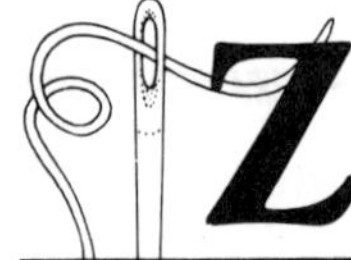

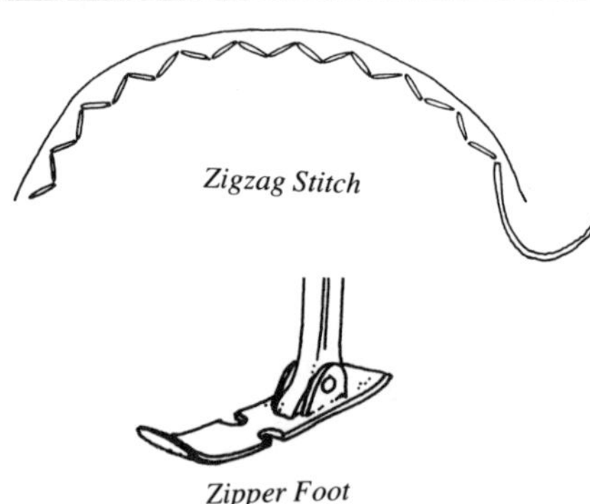

Zigzag Stitch

Zipper Foot

Zigzag Stitch: a machine stitch used for appliqué that is more open than a satin stitch.

Zipper Foot: a sewing machine attachment used for inserting zippers or for sewing on cording around the edge of a quilt. A zipper foot allows the needle to run very close to something that is bulky.

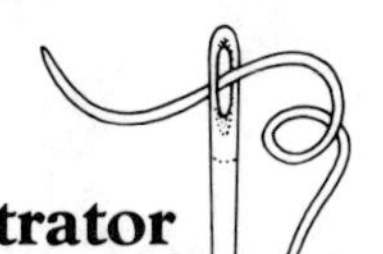

About the Author and Illustrator

Both Marie Shirer and Marla Stefanelli have enjoyed needlework and sewing since they were very young. They met in 1982, the year both joined the staff of Leman Publications, Inc., in Wheat Ridge, Colorado. Marie is Senior Editor of *Quilter's Newsletter Magazine* and the author of *Quilt Settings: A Workbook* (Moon Over the Mountain, 1989). Marla is an illustrator and designer for *Quilter's Newsletter Magazine* and *Quiltmaker*.

Recommended Reading

Family Keepsake Quilts by Vivian Howell Ritter is for anyone who wants to make a personalized memory quilt, a quilt that helps you say, "I was here and I cared about my family."

First Aid for Family Quilts by Nancy O'Bryant Puentes gives information on cleaning, restoring, documenting, and preserving quilts.

Handy-Crafts for Quilt Lovers by Georgianne Bender shows how to make gifts and decorator items using included quilt art.

How To Make a Quilt, 25 Easy Lessons for Beginners by Bonnie Leman and Louise O. Townsend shows how to make patchwork and appliqué quilts from start to finish.

Log Cabin Quilts by Bonnie Leman and Judy Martin is a comprehensive manual on a classic quilt style. Patterns, directions, and color photos.

Patchwork Sampler Legacy Quilt, Intermediate and Advanced Lessons in Patchwork by Bonnie Leman and *Quilter's Newsletter Magazine* staff gives patterns and quiltmaking lessons.

Quick & Cuddly Quilts by Theresa Eisinger features quilts and other projects for babies and children, all of which are easy to make.

Quilt Settings, A Workbook by Marie Shirer features many settings and patterns to be combined in creating hundreds of beautiful quilt designs.

Quilts: Visions of the World is a full-color collection of 77 original quilts made by artists in 14 countries.

The Rainbow Collection, Quilt Patterns for Rainbow Colors by Judy Martin offers 30 patterns, design inspiration, and color photos.

Scrap Quilts by Judy Martin offers techniques and patterns for typical yet unique scrap quilts and tips on collecting and organizing fabrics.

Shining Star Quilts, Lone Star Variations by Judy Martin presents comprehensive coverage of the history, techniques, and patterns for Sunbursts, Broken Stars, Blazing Stars, and more.

Taking the Math Out of Making Patchwork Quilts by Bonnie Leman and Judy Martin gives yardage and cutting charts for all patch shapes, settings, block, and quilt sizes.

Trapunto, The Handbook of Stuffed Quilting by Sue H. Rodgers offers complete instructions for embellishing quilts with a new, easy method of trapunto, with seven projects included.